ENTERING
into
FRIENDSHIP
with
GOD

ENTERING *into* FRIENDSHIP *with* GOD

An eight-week personal journey of prayer with the Word of God

Cristina Lima

Entering into Friendship with God

Copyright © 2019 by Cristina Lima.

All rights reserved. Printed in the United States.

No part of this publication may be reproduced, stored in a retrieval system, or transmitted in any form or by any means—electronic, mechanical, photocopying, recording, or otherwise—without written permission from the author except in the case of brief quotations embodied in critical articles and reviews.

For permissions information, contact:
cristinalima333@gmail.com

Copies of this book can be ordered at lulu.com.

Unless otherwise noted, scripture quotations are from the *New Revised Standard Version Bible: Catholic Edition* © 1989, 1993 Division of Christian Education of the National Council of the Churches of Christ in the United States of America. Used by permission. All rights reserved.

Scripture quotations marked with *NAB* are taken from the *New American Bible, revised edition* © 2010, 1991, 1986, 1970 Confraternity of Christian Doctrine, Washington, DC. and are used by permission of the copyright owner. All rights reserved. No part of the New American Bible may be reproduced in any form without permission in writing from the copyright owner.

Scripture quotations marked with *NIV* are taken from *The Holy Bible, New International Version® NIV®* © 1973, 1978, 1984, 2011 Biblica, Inc. Used by permission. All rights reserved worldwide.

"Invocation of Saint Michael the Archangel" is taken from *Prayers against the Powers of Darkness* © 2017 International Commission on English in the Liturgy Corporation, Washington, DC. All rights reserved.

Lord's Prayer, Nicene Creed, and other excerpts taken from the English translation of the *Catechism of the Catholic Church* © 1993 USCCB—Libreria Editrice Vaticana, Citta del Vaticano. All rights reserved.

Copyediting and Formatting: D Tinker Editing
www.balanceofseven.com/d-tinker-editing

Cover Design: Mark Gelotte
www.markgelotte.com

ISBN: 978-0-578-22454-1

Library of Congress Control Number: 2019912827

25 24 23 22 21 20 19   1 2 3 4 5

To my husband, Armando.
Together, we entered into relationship with God.
Our journeys are forever intertwined with our life commitment to
each other and to Christ.

To Patricia, Beatriz, Raquel, and Marcelo:
the most concrete expression of
our love for each other
and the love of God for us.

My lover speaks and says to me,
"Arise, my friend, my beautiful one,
and come!"

—Sg 2:10 (*NAB*)

Contents

Preface	xi
Acknowledgments	xv
Week 1: Praise	1
Week 2: Forgiveness	21
Week 3: Healing	41
Week 4: Prayer	69
Week 5: Word of God	93
Week 6: Service	119
Week 7: Sacraments	145
Week 8: Church	175

Preface

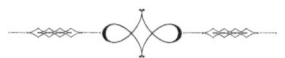

Entering into Friendship with God is a personal eight-week journey of daily reflections. It is designed for Catholics who are feeling a need to grow in their love, relationship, and friendship with God. It is written for you, no matter where you might be on your spiritual path. And because it is a personal and experiential journey, your takeaways from these reflections will follow your individual needs and desires.

Each week addresses a different topic that is fundamental to growing in intimacy with God. These topics are Praise, Forgiveness, Healing, Prayer, Word of God, Service, Sacraments, and the Church. Each day of the week is an invitation to explore different facets of the specific issue.

This is not a book to read and acquire knowledge from; it is a book to experience. The program should be completed in prayer. From the beginning, I invite you to open your heart and ask for wisdom and grace from the Holy Spirit. Topics and reflections are offered to motivate your heart, with the knowledge that reflections can go as deep as the heart of Jesus. All reflections are permeated with passages from the sacred scriptures, to be meditated on in the spirit of Lectio Divina.

Because this is a book to pray with, I recommend that you reserve at least twenty minutes each day for your reflection. Maybe you are already used to praying every day and this recommendation is not difficult for you. However, if you feel challenged by this commitment, do not worry. If twenty minutes is too much for you, start with ten minutes. If you cannot complete the daily reflection in one day, take two or three days to finish it. You will be fine. If you skip a day, do not give up. Resume your journey where you stopped and move on.

I also recommend that you follow the sequence of the book as there is a logical progression. However, if you would like to explore the topics out of sequence, you will still be fine.

This book is designed to provide space for you to write your thoughts, feelings, and experiences each day. However, some people might prefer to use a separate notebook for this purpose. Whether you use this book or a separate notebook, I recommend that you take the opportunity each day to write down your reflections. The process of writing down your thoughts not only helps you process them in the moment but also helps you evaluate your growth later on.

This eight-week journey represents the movement of the soul that happens in one moment of prayer as much as in a lifetime of prayer. As an ascending spiral, the movement of the soul repeats over and over, moving up as the soul enters into deeper and deeper levels of relationship with God. You may start the journey with the perception that you are simply a follower of Jesus, as many others are. As you deepen your relationship with God, you will find yourself growing in intimacy with Him and moving from believer to servant, from servant to friend, from friend to beloved.

The first movement is **Praise**, as you put yourself before God and recognize Him as your God. The next movement will take you into your inner self, where you will find your sins and your wounds and become aware of your need of **Forgiveness** and **Healing**. Once again, you will look back to God in **Prayer** and open your heart to listen to Him as He talks to you through the **Word of God**. After this encounter, your heart will be moved to **Service,** knowing that this is how you are called to express love. Along the way, since you cannot love on your own, you are called to reach for the gifts of the **Sacraments,** in which you will find the presence of Jesus, who heals, nourishes, and strengthens you. And as you experience the presence of Jesus in your life, you will discover that you, a beloved, will enter into friendship with God not alone but as **Church**, the beautiful bride of Christ who is called to participate in the intimate life of the Trinity.

This is the journey I invite you to take. Come, see, and taste. Let us find out how to enter into and grow in friendship with God and discover that Jesus, your beloved, is calling you to an intimate friendship with Him.

Acknowledgments

I am truly grateful for God's countless blessings in my life. I am especially grateful to God for calling me to and providing me with the means for sharing my spiritual journey, and I hope it will benefit at least one soul.

Also, I can't be grateful enough to Armando Lima, Nick and Sheila Stulak, Nadine Piño, Adriana Moreira, and Deacon Tom Ruck for their kindness in taking the time to read the manuscript and offer their valuable feedback.

And I am grateful to you, my reader, for accepting the invitation to embark on this journey.

Week 1

Praise

Let us praise him the more, since we cannot fathom him,
for greater is he than all his works;
Awesome indeed is the LORD,
and wonderful his power.
Lift up your voice to glorify the LORD
as much as you can, for there is still more.
Extol him with renewed strength,
do not grow weary, for you cannot fathom him.
(Sir 43:28–30, *NAB*)

Day 1

You and I were created to praise God. When we praise God, our beings come into harmony with Him as the Eternal Father and Creator of us all.

One of the greatest gifts God wants to give us is for us to discover the value of praising Him endlessly. He wants our lives to be ruled by our joyous acknowledgment of Him.

Let us begin by praying Psalm 89.

> ⁶*The heavens praise your marvels, LORD,*
> *your loyalty in the assembly of the holy ones.*
> ⁷*Who in the skies ranks with the LORD?*
> *Who is like the LORD among the sons of the gods?*
> ⁸*A God dreaded in the council of the holy ones,*
> *greater and more awesome than all those around him!*
> ⁹*LORD, God of hosts, who is like you?*
> *Mighty LORD, your faithfulness surrounds you.*
> ¹⁰*You rule the raging sea;*
> *you still its swelling waves.*
> ¹⁴*You have a mighty arm.*
> *Your hand is strong; your right hand is ever exalted.*
> ¹⁵*Justice and judgment are the foundations of your throne;*
> *mercy and faithfulness march before you.*
> ¹⁶*Blessed the people who know the war cry,*
> *who walk in the radiance of your face, LORD.*
> ¹⁷*In your name they sing joyfully all the day;*
> *they rejoice in your righteousness.* (Ps 89:6–10, 14–17, NAB)

Copy verse 17 on the next page, replacing the pronoun *they* with *I*.

Take a moment to ponder the meaning of this verse in your life today.

The Holy Spirit can make this verse become a reality in your life. He can teach you how to praise the Lord. Recall that Jesus said, "The holy Spirit . . . will teach you everything and remind you of all that I have said to you" (John 14:26).

It is a good idea to ask the Holy Spirit how to learn this practice of praising God.

Here's a prayer to ask the Holy Spirit for assistance:

> Come, Holy Spirit, teach me to praise the Lord; teach me to "sing joyfully all the day" in the presence of God. I easily nag and complain. It is so hard for me to surrender and praise with joy. Please, come and help me. Teach me the joys of praising the Lord. Please, give me the words and infuse my heart with Your Spirit.

I encourage you to pray to the Holy Spirit for guidance every day this week, as you begin each day and before you sleep at night. You can be assured of His grace and guidance.

Let us conclude this first day of praise with Psalm 135. Let this passage resonate within you for the rest of the day.

> *¹Hallelujah!*
> *Praise the name of the LORD!*

Praise, you servants of the LORD,
²Who stand in the house of the LORD,
in the courts of the house of our God!
³Praise the LORD, for the LORD is good!
Sing to his name, for it brings joy! (Ps 135:1–3, NAB)

What is the fruit of your reflection today?

_____

_____

_____

_____

_____

Day 2

To praise God is to pay Him the honor He deserves. After all, God is infinite love and is worthy of being praised for His unconditional love for us.

Let us prepare our hearts to pray with Psalm 136.

> *¹Praise the LORD, for he is good,*
> *for his mercy endures forever.*
> *²Praise the God of gods,*
> *for his mercy endures forever.*
> *³Praise the LORD of lords,*
> *for his mercy endures forever.* (Ps 136:1–3, *NAB*)

Let us praise the Lord with the following prayer exercise. Complete each sentence with praise to God for who He is. For example, "Lord, I praise You because You are good" (patient, merciful, etc.).

Lord, I praise You because You are _____.
Lord, I praise You because You are _____.
Lord, I praise You because You are _____.
Lord, I praise You because You are _____.
Lord, I praise You because You are _____.
Lord, I praise You because You are _____.
Lord, I praise You because You are _____.
Lord, I praise You because You are _____.

Of course, our words fall short in praising God's greatness. We are like children looking up at the night sky and trying to touch a star with our fingertips. Sometimes, we may be speechless. After all, God is so beyond our words, beyond our feelings. And aren't even our feelings sometimes hard to clarify, hard to articulate? Sometimes, we are muddled both in our thinking and in our feelings.

Yet we praise the Lord as a timid rehearsal for the reality of heaven, in which we will know Him face to face. For now, with our limited vocabulary, we can only try:

> Lord, I praise You because You are magnificent, almighty, the most high, holy and perfect, glorious and beautiful, fountain of love, light of the world, ever present, wise and powerful, merciful, kind, just, righteous, trustworthy, compassionate, patient, forgiving, consistent, Lord of lords, King of kings . . .

How do you feel in your heart when you praise the Lord?

_____
_____
_____
_____
_____

Let us finish this second day with a beautiful prayer from the Old Testament, taken from the book of Daniel. Let this passage be an inspiration for your prayers of praise.

> *[52] Blessed are you, O Lord, the God of our ancestors,*
> *praiseworthy and exalted above all forever;*
> *And blessed is your holy and glorious name,*
> *praiseworthy and exalted above all for all ages.*
> *[53] Blessed are you in the temple of your holy glory,*
> *praiseworthy and glorious above all forever.*
> *[54] Blessed are you on the throne of your kingdom,*
> *praiseworthy and exalted above all forever.*
> *[55] Blessed are you who look into the depths*
> *from your throne upon the cherubim,*

praiseworthy and exalted above all forever.
⁵⁶Blessed are you in the firmament of heaven,
praiseworthy and glorious forever. (Dn 3:52–56, *NAB*)

What is the fruit of your reflection today?

_____

_____

_____

_____

_____

Day 3

God is perfect love, and all He does is an expression of His merciful love. For this reason, He deserves to be praised not only for who He is but also for everything He does. God is perfect goodness, and all He does is good and worthy of praise and thanksgiving.

Let us start praying with Psalm 147.

> *¹Hallelujah!*
> *How good to sing praise to our God;*
> *how pleasant to give fitting praise.*
> *²The LORD rebuilds Jerusalem,*
> *and gathers the dispersed of Israel,*
> *³Healing the brokenhearted,*
> *and binding up their wounds.*
> *⁴He numbers the stars,*
> *and gives to all of them their names.*
> *⁵Great is our Lord, vast in power,*
> *with wisdom beyond measure.*
> *⁶The LORD gives aid to the poor,*
> *but casts the wicked to the ground.*
>
> *⁷Sing to the LORD with thanksgiving,*
> *with the lyre make music to our God.* (Ps 147:1–7, *NAB*)

Take a moment to praise the Lord with thanksgiving for all the good things He has done in your life. Ponder how God takes care of you. Also, consider that sometimes our perception of what happens to us can be clouded by our spiritual blindness. Sometimes we interpret "bad" circumstances as God not answering our prayers. Have you ever been disappointed that God didn't answer a prayer the way you wanted, but then later you realized that what did happen was so much better than what you had requested from God?

For this prayer exercise, list some reasons for you to be grateful to God for all He has done for you in the past and continues to do in the present. Don't forget to list those situations in which the blessings were at first misinterpreted as "bad" things.

>Lord, I praise You and give You thanks for:

_____
_____
_____
_____

With your heart full of thanksgiving, let us finish this third day of praise with the words of Psalm 66. Let this feeling of thanksgiving stay with you all day.

> *²Shout joyfully to God, all the earth;*
> *sing of his glorious name;*
> *give him glorious praise.*
> *³Say to God: "How awesome your deeds!*
> *Before your great strength your enemies cringe.*
> *⁴All the earth falls in worship before you,*
> *they sing of you, sing of your name!"*
>
> *⁵Come and see the works of God,*
> *awesome in deeds before the children of Adam.* (Ps 66:2–5, NAB)

What is the fruit of your reflection today?

_____
_____
_____
_____

Day 4

Those who praise God above all things find a precious treasure: trust in God.

This treasure can be seen in people's actions. For such a person, even if his heart is in sorrow, he still praises God. Even if the events of her life are disheartening, she continues praising God. To praise the Lord above all things means to surrender to God with trust, believing that He takes care of everything.

Haven't we all experienced moments when our lives seem to be nothing but series of disasters? Things go wrong, disappointments and arguments abound. It seems as if there were little going right.

At moments like this, let us locate the treasure of trust in God in our hearts. It is a life-affirming treasure that will guide us through the darkest of times on this earth. We can use the example of so many saints and martyrs, such as St. Faustina, St. John Paul II, St. Padre Pio, to inspire us to use this strategy.

Let us pray Psalm 138 as we prepare our hearts to praise God above everything.

> *[1b]I thank you, LORD, with all my heart;*
> *in the presence of the angels to you I sing.*
> *[2]I bow low toward your holy temple;*
> *I praise your name for your mercy and faithfulness.*
> *For you have exalted over all*
> *your name and your promise.*
> *[3]On the day I cried out, you answered;*
> *you strengthened my spirit.*
>
> *[7]Though I walk in the midst of dangers,*

you guard my life when my enemies rage.
You stretch out your hand;
your right hand saves me.
⁸The LORD is with me to the end.
LORD, your mercy endures forever.
Never forsake the work of your hands! (Ps 138:1b–3, 7–8, NAB)

Let your heart be full of praise, and trust in God's mercy. As you praise God in your heart, take a moment to offer Him your difficulties, sufferings, trials, and tribulations. By telling Him truthfully what your sorrows are, you take steps to establish a dialogue between you and God, which is often the definition of prayer.

In this prayer exercise, complete the paragraph below by listing what causes heaviness in your heart. Trust that God listens to your prayers.

> Jesus, I trust in You. I praise You amid my adversities. I offer all my difficulties and worries to You because You are my God. These are what I offer to You today, certain that You will receive them into Your hands and take care of each one of them:
>
> _____
> _____
> _____
> _____
> _____

Conclude the prayer with Psalm 34, to assure your heart that you can trust the Lord.

²I will bless the LORD at all times;
his praise shall be always in my mouth.
³My soul will glory in the LORD;
let the poor hear and be glad.
⁴Magnify the LORD with me;

and let us exalt his name together.

⁵I sought the LORD, and he answered me,
delivered me from all my fears.
⁶Look to him and be radiant,
and your faces may not blush for shame.
⁷This poor one cried out and the LORD heard,
and from all his distress he saved him. (Ps 34:2–7, NAB)

What is the fruit of your reflection today?

_____
_____
_____
_____
_____

Day 5

Praising God is not a matter of being "in the mood." Rather, praising God is simple recognition that God is good and takes care of everything for us, His very human and very fallible children.

Usually, we do not understand the way God works. In these moments, we need to trust Him more than ever.

Let us prepare our hearts today with a short passage from Matthew, which reminds us about trust.

> *[29] Are not two sparrows sold for a penny? Yet not one of them will fall to the ground apart from your Father. [30] And even the hairs of your head are all counted. [31] So do not be afraid; you are of more value than many sparrows.* (Mt 10:29–31)

For today's exercise, pray:

> Dear Jesus, I trust in You. Sometimes I feel joyful and confident, and sometimes I feel lost and scared. But You are always here for me; You are my haven. Teach me to be always in Your presence. Teach me to surrender to You all my joys and sorrows, with a heart full of praise and trust.

Close your eyes. Put yourself in the presence of God. Talk to Him with your own words and a sincere heart. Imagine Jesus receiving into His hands all that you have to offer today.

In the closing moments of your meditation time, read Romans 8:28 and keep it in mind throughout this day.

> *[28] We know that all things work together for good for those who love God, who are called according to his purpose.*

What is the fruit of your reflection today?

_____
_____
_____
_____
_____

Day 6

God does not need our praise. He is perfect; He has no needs. There is nothing that can be added to Him to make Him better or more complete.

But you and I do need to praise God in order to be whole human beings. We were created from a blueprint of praising God, and our souls only feel at home when we praise the Lord.

Let Psalm 63 speak to your heart today.

> *²O God, you are my God—*
> *it is you I seek!*
> *For you my body yearns;*
> *for you my soul thirsts,*
> *In a land parched, lifeless,*
> *and without water.*
> *³I look to you in the sanctuary*
> *to see your power and glory.*
> *⁴For your love is better than life;*
> *my lips shall ever praise you!* (Ps 63:2–4, NAB)

Ponder all the prayers, thoughts, and feelings of praise you have experienced this week since Day 1. Now write your own psalm of praise. It does not need to be perfect, but it is important that it comes from your heart.

_____

_____

_____

_____

_____
_____
_____
_____
_____

St. Paul wrote a letter to the Christian community in Ephesus and gave them advice that we can certainly take in our own lives. As we praise God in the name of Jesus, our hearts are freed to address our neighbors with a new joy.

The Word of God invites you to take this advice today and apply it to your life throughout this day.

> [18c]*Be filled with the Spirit,* [19]*as you sing psalms and hymns and spiritual songs among yourselves, singing and making melody to the Lord in your hearts,* [20]*giving thanks to God at all times and for everything in the name of our Lord Jesus Christ.* (Eph 5:18c–20)

What is the fruit of your reflection today?

_____
_____
_____
_____
_____

Day 7

The gift of praise is not for a moment of prayer only; rather, it is a gift for total life transformation.

Words of praise are meant to transform our lives into new lives of praise. In other words, praising God is not a prayer to be said at specific moments of the day; rather, it is an inner attitude of the heart. You might even say it is the core of the Christian way of life.

> *[16]Rejoice always, [17]pray without ceasing, [18]give thanks in all circumstances; for this is the will of God in Christ Jesus for you.*
> (1 Thes 5:16–18)

But you may ask, "How can I pray without ceasing?"

We all have busy lives: working, raising children, paying bills, etc. Yet this "pray[er] without ceasing" is the will of God for us. What, might we ask, is the "secret"? Do we all need to live in a monastery or seal ourselves off inside a hermit's cell? How can that be right?

The "secret" is that we are called to pray to God with words *and* with a transformed attitude toward life and others.

Pray Psalm 15 and ponder how praising God can be translated into loving others in your life.

> [1b]LORD, *who may abide in your tent?*
> *Who may dwell on your holy mountain?*
>
> [2]*Whoever walks without blame,*
> *doing what is right,*
> *speaking truth from the heart;*
> [3]*who does not slander with his tongue,*

does no harm to a friend,
never defames a neighbor. (Ps 15:1b–3, NAB)

As we conclude this first week, read the following passage from Philippians 4:4–9. It is a grace-filled summary of these reflections about praise.

> *⁴Rejoice in the Lord always; again I will say, Rejoice. ⁵Let your gentleness be known to everyone. The Lord is near. ⁶Do not worry about anything, but in everything by prayer and supplication with thanksgiving let your requests be made known to God. ⁷And the peace of God, which surpasses all understanding, will guard your hearts and your minds in Christ Jesus.*
>
> *⁸Finally, beloved, whatever is true, whatever is honorable, whatever is just, whatever is pure, whatever is pleasing, whatever is commendable, if there is any excellence and if there is anything worthy of praise, think about these things. ⁹Keep on doing the things that you have learned and received and heard and seen in me, and the God of peace will be with you.*

This week, you have reflected on and prayed about praise. Review your reflections from the week and write below what you learned that is new, surprising, or transformative.

_____
_____
_____
_____
_____
_____
_____
_____
_____

Week 2

Forgiveness

*If we confess our sins, he who is faithful and just
will forgive us our sins and cleanse us from all unrighteousness.*
(1 Jn 1:9)

*For if you forgive others their trespasses,
your heavenly Father will also forgive you.*
(Mt 6:14)

Day 1

God wants to fulfill our lives with His blessings and grace. It is His will to give us the inner peace we so need in our troubled lives. Isn't it true that sometimes all we need is peace in our hearts?

In His mercy, our loving Father indicates how to find the inner peace we so desire. One of the most precious ways to achieve inner peace is through forgiveness.

It is not an easy way, but it is a sure way. Read what the gospel teaches about forgiveness:

> *^{24}So I tell you, whatever you ask for in prayer, believe that you have received it, and it will be yours. ^{25}Whenever you stand praying, forgive, if you have anything against anyone; so that your Father in heaven may also forgive you your trespasses.* (Mk 11:24–25)

Forgiveness is so vital to Jesus that He also says:

> *^{23}So when you are offering your gift at the altar, if you remember that your brother or sister has something against you, ^{24}leave your gift there before the altar and go; first be reconciled to your brother or sister, and then come and offer your gift.* (Mt 5:23–24)

It sounds like a very strong statement, doesn't it? Well, that's how serious God is about forgiveness. Consider how the Word of God makes clear the importance of forgiveness.

Yet sometimes it can be so difficult to forgive. As you acknowledge your difficulties with forgiveness, read again Mark 11:24.

> *^{24}So I tell you, whatever you ask for in prayer, believe that you have received it, and it will be yours.*

In this first day of prayer and reflection on forgiveness, ask the Holy Spirit for the grace of forgiveness. Ask the Holy Spirit to come and teach you all about forgiveness. Let the Holy Spirit touch your heart and transform it into a forgiving one.

Begin praying:

> Dear Jesus, it is not always easy for me to forgive or ask for forgiveness, so I ask the Holy Spirit to come and help me. Come, Holy Spirit, teach me all about forgiveness, and touch my heart so I may have the disposition to forgive. Give me the grace I need to obey my Lord Jesus, who commands me to forgive. Let me experience the inner peace that comes with forgiveness. Prepare my heart for this week of prayer and reflection on forgiveness. Amen.

Once you've completed your prayer asking for the gift of forgiveness, trust that your petition has been heard.

Conclude your reflection by letting this passage be with you for the rest of this day:

> ^{9}*Do not lie to one another, seeing that you have stripped off the old self with its practices* ^{10}*and have clothed yourselves with the new self, which is being renewed in knowledge according to the image of its creator.*
>
> ^{12}*As God's chosen ones, holy and beloved, clothe yourselves with compassion, kindness, humility, meekness, and patience.* ^{13}*Bear with one another and, if anyone has a complaint against another, forgive each other; just as the Lord has forgiven you, so you also must forgive.*
> (Col 3:9–10, 12–13)

What is the fruit of your reflection today?

_____

_____

_____

_____

Day 2

Let us continue our reflection on forgiveness. Begin by taking some time to present yourself before God with a humble heart. Close your eyes and ask forgiveness for your own sins, particularly for the sin of lacking forgiveness.

Psalm 51 is especially inspiring in preparing your heart for this prayer.

> ^{1}*Have mercy on me, O God,*
>   *according to your unfailing love;*
> *according to your great compassion*
>   *blot out my transgressions.*
> ^{2}*Wash away all my iniquity;*
>   *and cleanse me from my sin.*
>
> ^{3}*For I know my transgressions;*
>   *and my sin is always before me.*
> ^{4}*Against you, you only, have I sinned*
>   *and done what is evil in your sight,*
> *so you are right in your verdict*
>   *and justified when you judge.*
> ^{5}*Surely I was sinful at birth,*
>   *sinful from the time my mother conceived me.*
> ^{6}*Yet you desired faithfulness even in the womb;*
>   *you taught me wisdom in that secret place.*
>
> ^{7}*Cleanse me with hyssop, and I will be clean;*
>   *wash me, and I will be whiter than snow.*
> ^{8}*Let me hear joy and gladness;*
>   *let the bones you have crushed rejoice.* (Ps 51:1–8, *NIV*)

When we do not forgive others, we first sin against God, because He has ordered us to forgive. With a humble heart, continue your prayer:

> Forgive me, Lord, for I do not forgive very easily. I tend to hold grudges against others and ruminate upon resentments in my heart. I know Your will for me, and my lack of forgiveness is a sin against You. I tend to hold onto self-pity and cherish the hurtful things that were done to me, as excuses for hatred and revenge. Help me, God. Have mercy on me and forgive me. Give me a more forgiving heart, according to Your will.

This is what God tells you after your humble and sincere prayer:

> ^{1b}*Blessed is the one whose fault is removed,*
> *whose sin is forgiven.*
> ^{2}*Blessed is the man to whom the LORD imputes no guilt,*
> *in whose spirit is no deceit.* (Ps 32:1b–2, NAB)

What is the fruit of your reflection today?

_____
_____
_____
_____
_____

Day 3

Forgiveness is an order from God, but it is also a necessity for us. We need to forgive. Our hearts were not created to hold grudges, resentment, or hatred. Our hearts were created for love.

When we do not love, we fall ill in our souls, bodies, and minds. The lack of forgiveness distances us from God and from others and throws our inner selves out of balance. Forgiveness is key to a fulfilled life in God.

Some people find it difficult to forgive because they think forgiveness is a feeling. However, forgiveness does not depend on feelings. Forgiving is an act of will. It is purposefully willing good for the other person.

One forgives because one decides and wants to forgive in obedience to God.

The act of forgiving is a deeply liberating act. You may not feel anything in the moment other than the peace and joy of doing God's will. Simply praying for the other person is the first step in forgiveness.

Some who have suffered serious traumatic experiences, such as abuse or attempts against their physical or psychological integrity, may have difficulty forgiving their offenders. They might think that forgiving requires them to accept what has been done to them or that, after forgiveness, they must have a relationship with the person who offended them.

This is not what Jesus said. Forgiveness does not change whether an act is wrong. And there are situations in which physical reconciliation and proximity are not recommended at all. Yet forgiveness can be attained and is necessary to free the heart from hurt and pain.

Today, I encourage you to forgive the person who has offended you the most. To prepare your heart, pray with this parable from Matthew 18:23–35 (*NIV*).

> *²³Therefore, the kingdom of heaven is like a king who wanted to settle accounts with his servants. ²⁴As he began the settlement, a man who owed him ten thousand bags of gold was brought to him. ²⁵Since he was not able to pay, the master ordered that he and his wife and his children and all that he had be sold to repay the debt. ²⁶At this the servant fell on his knees before him. "Be patient with me," he begged, "and I will pay back everything." ²⁷The servant's master took pity on him, canceled the debt and let him go. ²⁸But when that servant went out, he found one of his fellow servants who owed him a hundred silver coins. He grabbed him and began to choke him. "Pay back what you owe me!" he demanded. ²⁹His fellow servant fell to his knees and begged him, "Be patient with me, and I will pay it back." ³⁰But he refused. Instead, he went off and had the man thrown into prison until he could pay the debt. ³¹When the other servants saw what had happened, they were outraged and went and told their master everything that had happened. ³²Then the master called the servant in. "You wicked servant," he said, "I canceled all that debt of yours because you begged me to. ³³Shouldn't you have had mercy on your fellow servant just as I had on you?" ³⁴In anger his master handed him over to the jailers to be tortured, until he should pay back all he owed. ³⁵This is how my heavenly Father will treat each of you unless you forgive your brother or sister from your heart.*

Inspired by this parable, think about the person who has deliberately offended you. Pray:

> Dear Jesus, I come to You today to pray about my need to forgive [say the name of the person]. I ask You for the gift of forgiveness because it is very difficult for me to forgive. I cannot do it without Your help or Your grace. Due to my pain, I may not feel the forgiveness, but in obedience to You and with Your grace, I trust You, and I want to say the

words of forgiveness. Jesus, in Your name, I forgive [say the name of the person] for all the pain and suffering afflicted on me. I trust that my forgiveness frees my heart of all resentment, hatred, and pain. Thank You, Lord, for helping me to forgive and for healing my heart.

Continue your prayer, telling God how you feel. You can open your heart and be honest with God. He understands you and wants to fill your heart with peace.

This prayer of forgiveness may be difficult for you. If this is the case, close your eyes and hold Jesus's hands until the Holy Spirit pacifies your heart. If this prayer is too overwhelming for you, please consider speaking with someone you trust, like a priest or a professional counselor. Even though resolution may not happen right away, trust that Jesus will not give up. He will ultimately bring you freedom from the inside out.

May these words from John be with you for the rest of this day:

> *[27]Peace I leave with you; my peace I give to you. I do not give to you as the world gives. Do not let your hearts be troubled, and do not let them be afraid.* (Jn 14:27)

What is the fruit of your reflection today?

_____
_____
_____
_____
_____

Day 4

Yesterday, your reflection and prayer were about forgiving the person who has offended you the most. Today, I invite you to forgive all others who may have offended you or caused you some kind of pain in the past but who may not have intended to harm you.

Think about your parents, siblings, teachers, friends, and other people with whom you may have had conflicts, arguments, or disagreements. Perhaps there are people who offended you in the past against whom you still hold resentment. Maybe it is difficult for you to let go of the bitterness that gets stuck in your memory.

Today, I encourage you to seek healing for all the lack of forgiveness you have been holding in your heart for years. Today is the day to hand over to God all bitterness, anger, and desires of revenge that you carry within your heart, and to let the Holy Spirit replace them with blessings.

> [2]*Forgive your neighbor the wrong done to you;*
> *then when you pray, your own sins will be forgiven.*
> [3]*Does anyone nourish anger against another*
> *and expect healing from the LORD?*
> [4]*Can one refuse mercy to a sinner like oneself,*
> *yet seek pardon for one's own sins?*
> [7]*Remember the commandments and do not be angry with your neighbor;*
> *remember the covenant of the Most High, and overlook faults.*
> (Sir 28:2–4, 7, NAB)

> [9]*Do not repay evil for evil or abuse for abuse; but, on the contrary, repay with a blessing. It is for this that you were called—that you might inherit a blessing.* (1 Pt 3:9)

Begin praying:

> Dear God, I come to You today because I need healing for all my lack of forgiveness. In many situations, I have kept resentment and bitterness in my heart. I ask forgiveness for my lack of forgiveness, and once again I ask Your help to forgive all those who have offended me in the past. In the name of Jesus, I forgive [list the names of the people who have offended you in the past]. I forgive them, and I ask You to bless them. Amen.

Continue your prayer with your own words, forgiving and requesting blessings for each person who comes to mind.

To complete your prayer today, let the Holy Spirit free your heart from all lack of forgiveness and transform your heart anew. Trust that God is merciful and powerful enough to give you a new heart. God can transform a dry and bitter heart into a loving and forgiving one. Ask for and accept this gift. Pray with this passage:

> *[18] Remember not the events of the past,*
> *the things of long ago consider not;*
> *[19] See, I am doing something new!*
> *Now it springs forth, do you not perceive it?*
> *In the wilderness I make a way,*
> *in the wasteland, rivers.*
> *[20] Wild beasts honor me,*
> *jackals and ostriches,*
> *For I put water in the wilderness*
> *and rivers in the wasteland*
> *for my chosen people to drink.* (Is 43:18–20, *NAB*)

What is the fruit of your reflection today?

_____

_____

_____

Day 5

There is no doubt of the importance that Jesus places on forgiveness. It is also clear that forgiveness is not a one-time deal, but a constant work-in-progress and disposition of the heart.

> *²¹Then Peter came and said to him, "Lord, if another member of the church sins against me, how often should I forgive? As many as seven times?" ²²Jesus said to him, "Not seven times, but, I tell you, seventy-seven times." (Mt 18:21–22)*

Today, I invite you to forgive those who offend you over and over in the present day.

These would be people who are difficult to be around but whom you cannot avoid completely. Think about your boss, coworkers, neighbors, and family members. It could be someone you love, like your husband or wife, who may say or do certain things you cannot stand.

Maybe they offend you on purpose. Or maybe you get annoyed with the way they are, which is a lack of acceptance translating into a lack of forgiveness.

Maybe you express your lack of forgiveness by being aggressive toward others, either with words or acts. Or maybe you do not express your anger toward others but keep the bitterness trapped in your heart, making you feel miserable.

Whatever the situation, you cannot keep carrying these angry and bitter feelings in your heart. Today is the day to give them over to God by forgiving and accepting people who are part of your everyday life.

Begin praying:

My sweet Jesus, You accept me the way I am. Help me forgive those who offend me in my everyday life, and help me accept those around me the way they are. In Your name, Jesus, and with the help of the Holy Spirit, I forgive [say the name of the people] for all distress they cause in my life. I forgive them with all my heart, and I ask You to bless them. Give me the wisdom to avoid unnecessary conflicts and to be kinder and more flexible. Give me the discernment to know when it is wise to speak up and when it is wise to keep silent. Dear Jesus, remind me to keep forgiving them as You forgive me my everyday flaws. Thank You for being with me and for giving me the inner peace I so need. Amen.

Continue this prayer with your own words. When done, read the following passages and let them inspire your day.

> *[31] Put away from you all bitterness and wrath and anger and wrangling and slander, together with all malice, [32] and be kind to one another, tenderhearted, forgiving one another, as God in Christ has forgiven you.* (Eph 4:31–32)

> *[9] Let love be genuine; hate what is evil, hold fast to what is good; [10] love one another with mutual affection; outdo one another in showing honor. [11] Do not lag in zeal, be ardent in spirit, serve the Lord. [12] Rejoice in hope, be patient in suffering, persevere in prayer. [13] Contribute to the needs of the saints; extend hospitality to strangers. [14] Bless those who persecute you; bless and do not curse them. [15] Rejoice with those who rejoice, weep with those who weep. [16] Live in harmony with one another; do not be haughty, but associate with the lowly; do not claim to be wiser than you are. [17] Do not repay anyone evil for evil, but take thought for what is noble in the sight of all. [18] If it is possible, so far as it depends on you, live peaceably with all. [19] Beloved, never avenge yourselves, but leave room for the wrath of God; for it is written, "Vengeance is mine, I will repay, says the Lord." [20] No, "if your enemies are hungry, feed them; if they are thirsty, give them something to drink; for*

by doing this you will heap burning coals on their heads." ²¹Do not be overcome by evil, but overcome evil with good. (Rom 12:9–21)

What is the fruit of your reflection today?

_____
_____
_____
_____
_____

Day 6

The Word of God testifies that God is good and just and that there is no fault or deceit in all His deeds. Listen and instill this truth in your heart once and for all with this passage:

> *^{1}Give ear, O heavens, and let me speak;*
> *let the earth hear the words of my mouth!*
> *^{2}May my teaching soak in like the rain,*
> *and my utterance drench like the dew.*
> *Like a downpour upon the grass,*
> *like a shower upon the crops.*
> *^{3}For I will proclaim the name of the LORD,*
> *praise the greatness of our God!*
>
> *^{4}The Rock—how faultless are his deeds,*
> *how right all his ways!*
> *A faithful God, without deceit,*
> *just and upright is he!* (Dt 32:1–4, *NAB*)

Even though God is good, some people turn against Him when unwanted events happen in their lives. They revolt against God because they do not understand why God could let bad things happen to them. They blame God for the choices other people make and ignore the fact that God created us with free will.

> *^{11}Do not say: "It was God's doing that I fell away,"*
> *for that he hates he does not do.*
> *^{12}Do not say: "He himself has led me astray,"*
> *for he has no need of the wicked.*
> *^{13}Abominable wickedness the LORD hates*
> *and he does not let it happen to those who fear him.*

> *¹⁴God in the beginning created human beings
> and made them subject to their own free choice.* (Sir 15:11–14, *NAB*)

You may have experienced situations in which, in pain, you revolted against God for letting something happen to you or to someone dear to you. Maybe you held resentment against God, not fully realizing what you were doing.

Because God has not done anything wrong, He does not need forgiveness. However, you may need to give forgiveness to God for your own benefit, as a way to free your heart from resentment you might be holding against Him.

Today, I invite you to pray:

> Dear God, I trust in Your perfect love, and I praise You for Your everlasting goodness. I come to You today to ask forgiveness for the times I have lost trust in You and held resentment against You. You do not need my forgiveness, but I need to say the words. I forgive You, my God, for letting [if possible, be specific] happen to me (or to someone dear to me). I was upset and mad at You because You let this happen. Now I understand my foolishness, and I want to be completely reconciled with You. Thank You for delivering me from all animosity against You so I can love You with all my heart. From now on, I will always trust You. Amen.

God does not hold anything against you. On the contrary, He has waited for you to celebrate a complete reconciliation with Him. He says:

> *²⁰Listen! I am standing at the door, knocking; if you hear my voice and open the door, I will come in to you and eat with you, and you with me.* (Rev 3:20)

To finish today's reflection, let this passage inspire you to greater trust in God:

⁷You that fear the Lord, wait for his mercy,
do not stray lest you fall.
⁸You that fear the Lord, trust in him,
and your reward will not be lost.
⁹You that fear the LORD, hope for good things,
for lasting joy and mercy. (Sir 2:7–9, NAB)

What is the fruit of your reflection today?

_____
_____
_____
_____
_____

Day 7

You are deeply loved by God. You are precious to the Lord. He loves you and forgives you your sins. He accepts you just the way you are and wants to fill your life with His love.

Read the following passage from Isaiah and let the Word of God convince your soul of the immeasurable love God has for you.

> *¹But now, thus says the LORD,*
> *who created you, Jacob, and formed you, Israel:*
> *Do not fear, for I have redeemed you;*
> *I have called you by name: you are mine.*
> *²When you pass through waters, I will be with you;*
> *through rivers, you shall not be swept away.*
> *When you walk through fire, you shall not be burned,*
> *nor will flames consume you.*
> *³For I, the LORD, am your God,*
> *the Holy One of Israel, your savior.*
> *I give Egypt as ransom for you,*
> *Ethiopia and Seba in exchange for you.*
> *⁴Because you are precious in my eyes*
> *and honored, and I love you.* (Is 43:1–4, NAB)

Read the passage again, saying your name in place of Jacob and Israel.

Now, complete the following sentence with your name and read it several times. Listen with your heart to what God is telling you now.

> My beloved _____, you are precious in My eyes, and I love you.

Take some time to ponder this: considering that God loves and accepts you the way you are, is it fair to conclude that you are called to love and accept yourself in the same way?

Jesus said, "You shall love your neighbor as yourself" (Mt 22:39). Does this not imply that God wants you to love yourself? The truth is, God wants you to love yourself as He loves and accepts you.

It is very difficult to truly love and forgive others if one does not love and forgive oneself.

Today, you are invited to forgive yourself and free yourself from the guilt, remorse, and ruminations over your own flaws and limitations.

Let the Holy Spirit accomplish in your life a deep inner healing through the grace of self-forgiveness and acceptance.

> *[18] Come now, let us set things right,*
> *says the LORD:*
> *Though your sins be like scarlet,*
> *they may become white as snow;*
> *Thought they be red like crimson,*
> *they may become white as wool.*
> *[19] If you are willing, and obey,*
> *you shall eat the good things of the land.* (Is 1:18–19, *NAB*)

I invite you to pray:

> My Lord, I know You love me and accept me as I am. I am deeply grateful because You forgive me my sins and want to accomplish wonders in my life. Dear Jesus, once again I ask forgiveness for my sins and for not responding to Your love as I should. Today, I come to You and ask Your help to reconcile with myself. In Your name, I forgive myself for my sins and wrongdoings, and I hand over to You my guilt, my shame, my self-accusation, and my remorse. Today, I want to be free of everything I hold against myself. I forgive myself for [be specific] because You have forgiven me. Lord, I accept Your forgiveness and love, and I hold Your

hand as I forgive myself and accept myself as You do. Thank You, Lord, for Your love, forgiveness, and healing. Amen.

As you conclude your prayer today, keep these words with you for the rest of the day:

^{1}Happy those whose mouth causes them no grief, those who are not stung by remorse for sin.
^{2}Happy are those whose conscience does not reproach them, those who have not lost hope. (Sir 14:1–2, NAB)

Dear God, thank You for teaching me about forgiveness and for giving me the opportunity to practice Your Word. Thank You for the blessings and healing I have received as I've prayed on the topic of forgiveness. Amen.

This week, you have reflected on and prayed about forgiveness. Review your reflections from the week and write below what you learned that is new, surprising, or transformative.

_____
_____
_____
_____
_____
_____
_____
_____
_____

Week 3

Healing

Many crowds followed him, and he cured all of them.
(Mt 12:15)

I am the LORD who heals you.
(Ex 15:26)

Day 1

Our God is our healer and our savior.

Healing and salvation are the same for Jesus. According to the Gospels, Jesus heals all who come to Him; He saves everyone from sin, spiritual bondage, and physical and psychological afflictions.

He wants to heal us at our cores, saving us completely from everything, from spiritual death to physical and emotional distress.

Healing is central to Jesus's mission. Jesus was recognized as the Messiah because of the healings He performed.

> ^{18b}So John summoned two of his disciples ^{19}and sent them to the Lord to ask, "Are you the one who is to come, or are we to wait for another?" ^{20}When the men had come to him, they said, "John the Baptist has sent us to you to ask, 'Are you the one who is to come, or are we to wait for another?'" ^{21}Jesus had just then cured many people of diseases, plagues, and evil spirits, and had given sight to many who were blind. ^{22}And he answered them, "Go and tell John what you have seen and heard: the blind receive their sight, the lame walk, the lepers are cleansed, the deaf hear, the dead are raised, the poor have good news brought to them. ^{23}And blessed is anyone who takes no offense at me." (Lk 7:18b–23)

As we can see, Jesus presents Himself as our healer.

Now, read the following passage about the ministry of Jesus and answer the questions on the next page.

> ^{23}Jesus went throughout Galilee, teaching in their synagogues and proclaiming the good news of the kingdom and curing every disease and every sickness among the people. ^{24}So his fame spread throughout all

> *Syria, and they brought to him all the sick, those who were afflicted with various diseases and pains, demoniacs, epileptics, and paralytics, and he cured them.* (Mt 4:23–24)

According to verse 23, what diseases did Jesus cure?

___

According to verse 24, who did Jesus cure?

___

Considering that Jesus healed all who were sick, of every disease, and considering that "Jesus Christ is the same yesterday and today and forever" (Heb 13:8), is there any reason to think that God would treat you any differently?

Read the following texts to discover what you need to do to receive the healing you are looking for.

> *^{40}A leper came to him begging him, and kneeling he said to him, "If you choose, you can make me clean." ^{41}Moved with pity, Jesus stretched out his hand and touched him, and said to him, "I do choose. Be made clean!" ^{42}Immediately the leprosy left him, and he was made clean.* (Mk 1:40–42)

> *^{30}There were two blind men sitting by the roadside. When they heard that Jesus was passing by, they shouted, "Lord, have mercy on us, Son of David!" ^{31}The crowd sternly ordered them to be quiet; but they shouted even more loudly, "Have mercy on us, Lord, Son of David!" ^{32}Jesus stood still and called them, saying, "What do you want me to do for you?" ^{33}They said to him, "Lord, let our eyes be opened." ^{34}Moved with compassion, Jesus touched their eyes. Immediately they regained their sight and followed him.* (Mt 20:30–34)

The leper approached Jesus with faith and humility and begged. The blind men cried out for compassion and were not afraid to say what they wanted Jesus to do for them.

Inspired by these passages, take some time today to approach Jesus and beg: "Lord, if You wish, You can heal me. Have mercy on me." Then tell Jesus what you want. Listen to Jesus telling you with compassion, "I hear you. Be healed."

What is the fruit of your reflection today?

_____
_____
_____
_____
_____

Day 2

It is Jesus's mission to save (heal) you from all that stands between you and the full life God has planned for you.

One important healing that Jesus wants to give you is healing from your sins. They are spiritual illnesses that take you away from God.

Today, I invite you to consider your sins and pray, asking God to deliver you from all your iniquities. As a preparation for this moment, pray with Psalm 25 (*NIV*).

> *¹In you, LORD my God,*
>   *I put my trust.*
>
> *²I trust in you;*
>   *do not let me be put to shame,*
>   *nor let my enemies triumph over me.*
> *³No one who hopes in you*
>   *will ever be put to shame,*
> *but shame will come on those*
>   *who are treacherous without cause.*
>
> *⁴Show me your ways, LORD,*
>   *teach me your paths.*
> *⁵Guide me in your truth and teach me,*
>   *for you are God my Savior,*
>   *and my hope is in you all day long.*
> *⁶Remember, LORD, your great mercy and love,*
>   *for they are from of old.*
> *⁷Do not remember the sins of my youth*
>   *and my rebellious ways;*
> *according to your love remember me,*

for you, LORD, are good.
⁸Good and upright is the LORD;
therefore he instructs sinners in his ways.
⁹He guides the humble in what is right
and teaches them his way.
¹⁰All the ways of the LORD are loving and faithful
toward those who keep the demands of his covenant.
¹¹For the sake of your name, LORD,
forgive my iniquity, though it is great.

¹²Who, then, are those who fear the LORD?
He will instruct them in the ways they should choose.
¹³They will spend their days in prosperity,
and their descendants will inherit the land.
¹⁴The LORD confides in those who fear him;
he makes his covenant known to them.
¹⁵My eyes are ever on the LORD,
for only he will release my feet from the snare.

¹⁶Turn to me and be gracious to me,
for I am lonely and afflicted.
¹⁷Relieve the troubles of my heart
and free me from my anguish.
¹⁸Look on my affliction and my distress
and take away all my sins.
¹⁹See how numerous are my enemies
and how fiercely they hate me!

²⁰Guard my life and rescue me;
do not let me be put to shame,
for I take refuge in you.
²¹May integrity and uprightness protect me,
because my hope, LORD, is in you.

²²Deliver Israel, O God,
from all their troubles!

Do you believe Jesus can free you from your sins and their consequences in your life? Do you believe He can free you and give you a completely new and transformed life?

Ponder the following passage.

> *¹⁷One day, while he was teaching, Pharisees and teachers of the law were sitting near by (they had come from every village of Galilee and Judea and from Jerusalem); and the power of the Lord was with him to heal. ¹⁸Just then some men came, carrying a paralyzed man on a bed. They were trying to bring him in and lay him before Jesus; ¹⁹but finding no way to bring him in because of the crowd, they went up on the roof and let him down with his bed through the tiles into the middle of the crowd in front of Jesus. ²⁰When he saw their faith, he said, "Friend, your sins are forgiven you." ²¹Then the scribes and the Pharisees began to question, "Who is this who is speaking blasphemies? Who can forgive sins but God alone?" ²²When Jesus perceived their questionings, he answered them, "Why do you raise such questions in your hearts? ²³Which is easier, to say, 'Your sins are forgiven you,' or to say, 'Stand up and walk'? ²⁴But so that you may know that the Son of Man has authority on earth to forgive sins"—he said to the one who was paralyzed—"I say to you, stand up and take your bed and go to your home." ²⁵Immediately he stood up before them, took what he had been lying on, and went to his home, glorifying God. ²⁶Amazement seized all of them, and they glorified God and were filled with awe, saying, "We have seen strange things today." (Lk 5:17–26)*

How does your soul react to this reflection? How can you respond to God?

_____
_____
_____
_____
_____

Healing 49

Now pray:

> Dear Jesus, I come to You today in need of healing from my sins. You are God, and You can save me from my sins. I come to You humbly with the little faith I have, trusting in Your mercy. My soul is crippled by my sins. Some of my sins affect my life in such a way that I feel trapped, and I have difficulty getting rid of them on my own. I need Your help. Please, forgive me and heal me of all my sins, including those I do not remember right now. I also ask forgiveness and healing of the sins I want to get rid of but keep falling into over and over. I can't do it on my own. I need Your help with these: [name these sins]. I also need help with the sins I have difficulty letting go of because they provide me with some sort of satisfaction. I need special help with these: [name these sins]. Please, take away all my sins. Dear Jesus, come to me and touch my soul with Your mercy and heal my heart so I can change my life and love You more. Thank You, Jesus. I trust in You. Amen.

Take some time today to think about your sins and make a firm commitment to go to confession. As you prepare for confession with a humble and sincere heart, trust that God forgives you and grants you a new beginning.

The sacrament of confession is the seal of God's forgiveness and healing.

Complete your reflection today with this text from Luke. Let this passage be an inspiration for you to replace your sins with thanksgiving to and love for our merciful and compassionate God.

> *[36] One of the Pharisees asked Jesus to eat with him, and he went into the Pharisee's house and took his place at the table. [37] And a woman in the city, who was a sinner, having learned that he was eating in the Pharisee's house, brought an alabaster jar of ointment. [38] She stood behind him at his feet, weeping, and began to bathe his feet with her*

tears and to dry them with her hair. Then she continued kissing his feet and anointing them with the ointment. ³⁹*Now when the Pharisee who had invited him saw it, he said to himself, "If this man were a prophet, he would have known who and what kind of woman this is who is touching him—that she is a sinner."* ⁴⁰*Jesus spoke up and said to him, "Simon, I have something to say to you." "Teacher," he replied, "speak."* ⁴¹ *"A certain creditor had two debtors; one owed five hundred denarii, and the other fifty.* ⁴²*When they could not pay, he canceled the debts for both of them. Now which of them will love him more?"* ⁴³*Simon answered, "I suppose the one for whom he canceled the greater debt." And Jesus said to him, "You have judged rightly."* ⁴⁴*Then turning toward the woman, he said to Simon, "Do you see this woman? I entered your house; you gave me no water for my feet, but she has bathed my feet with her tears and dried them with her hair.* ⁴⁵*You gave me no kiss, but from the time I came in she has not stopped kissing my feet.* ⁴⁶*You did not anoint my head with oil, but she has anointed my feet with ointment.* ⁴⁷*Therefore, I tell you, her sins, which were many, have been forgiven; hence she has shown great love. But the one to whom little is forgiven, loves little."* ⁴⁸*Then he said to her, "Your sins are forgiven."* ⁴⁹*But those who were at the table with him began to say among themselves, "Who is this who even forgives sins?"* ⁵⁰*And he said to the woman, "Your faith has saved you; go in peace."* (Lk 7:36–50)

As you finish your reflection and prayer, write your name in the blank space below. Listen to what Jesus tells you today. Keep these words with you.

_____, your faith has saved you; go in peace.

What is the fruit of your reflection today?

_____
_____
_____
_____

Day 3

When Jesus taught us the Lord's Prayer, He taught us to ask for deliverance from evil, a deep spiritual healing that He wants to perform in our lives.

> *^{13}And do not bring us to the time of trial,
> but rescue us from the evil one.* (Mt 6:13)

The evil one is a spiritual reality we experience every day. Yesterday, you experienced the healing of your sins. Today, I encourage you to experience healing from the evil one.

> *^{32}That evening, at sunset, they brought to him all who were sick or possessed with demons. ^{33}And the whole city was gathered around the door. ^{34}And he cured many who were sick with various diseases, and cast out many demons; and he would not permit the demons to speak, because they knew him.* (Mk 1:32–34)

There are levels of evil influence. The first level is temptation. Even Jesus was tempted (see Mt 4:1–11). We are constantly tempted to fall into sin. We need help from God to say no to the temptations we experience.

Then there is the level at which we consent to evil spirits entering our lives, even when we might not be aware of our consent. This level of evil influence can happen when we commit mortal sins, especially those that keep us enslaved, such as addictions and compulsive sins of violence and sexual nature.

We can also give our consent to evil spirits by engaging in occult practices. Even "innocent" practices can act as consent for evil spirits to enter into our lives. These practices might include horoscopes, fortune-telling, and tarot. At this level, the evil influence distances our minds from God, weakens our faith, and creates obstacles to conversion.

The next level is more serious. It happens when a person deliberately looks for an occult experience and becomes possessed by evil spirits. In this reflection and prayer, we will focus only on the first and second levels of the influence of evil. If you think you are being possessed or tormented by evil spirits in a deeper way, you should speak with your pastor. God wants to deliver the possessed ones, but they need personal assistance for that.

Now, as you prepare for today's healing, ponder Jesus's authority and willingness to save us from evil spirits.

Read the following examples of spiritual healing.

> *³¹He went down to Capernaum, a city in Galilee, and was teaching them on the sabbath. ³²They were astounded at his teaching, because he spoke with authority. ³³In the synagogue there was a man who had the spirit of an unclean demon, and he cried out with a loud voice, ³⁴"Let us alone! What have you to do with us, Jesus of Nazareth? Have you come to destroy us? I know who you are, the Holy One of God." ³⁵But Jesus rebuked him, saying, "Be silent, and come out of him!" When the demon had thrown him down before them, he came out of him without having done him any harm. ³⁶They were all amazed and kept saying to one another, "What kind of utterance is this? For with authority and power he commands the unclean spirits, and out they come!" ³⁷And a report about him began to reach every place in the region.* (Lk 4:31–37)

> *¹⁰Now he was teaching in one of the synagogues on the sabbath. ¹¹And just then there appeared a woman with a spirit that had crippled her for eighteen years. She was bent over and was quite unable to stand up straight. ¹²When Jesus saw her, he called her over and said, "Woman, you are set free from your ailment." ¹³When he laid his hands on her, immediately she stood up straight and began praising God. ¹⁴But the leader of the synagogue, indignant because Jesus had cured on the*

sabbath, kept saying to the crowd, "There are six days on which work ought to be done; come on those days and be cured, and not on the sabbath day." ¹⁵But the Lord answered him and said, "You hypocrites! Does not each of you on the sabbath untie his ox or his donkey from the manger, and lead it away to give it water? ¹⁶And ought not this woman, a daughter of Abraham whom Satan bound for eighteen long years, be set free from this bondage on the sabbath day?" ¹⁷When he said this, all his opponents were put to shame; and the entire crowd was rejoicing at all the wonderful things that he was doing. (Lk 13:10–17)

Assured that Jesus wants to free you from all evil that holds you, begin praying:

> My dear God, I come to You today to ask for spiritual healing. I proclaim Jesus as my Lord and Savior, who comes to my rescue in times of peril. Please, Lord Jesus, deliver me from the evil one and set me free from all spiritual chains that bind me. I ask Your forgiveness for the times I have given consent for evil spirits to enter into my life. I humbly ask You forgiveness for my sins of idolatry and occult practices, such as [be specific], even though I committed them in ignorance, unaware of the spiritual reality behind them. In the name of Jesus, I solemnly renounce the participation of any evil spirits in my life and any benefits I have received from them. I ask You, my Lord, for the gift of discernment so I can immediately recognize evil and flee from it. Thank You, Jesus, for healing my soul, delivering me from all evil influence, and setting me free to love You. Amen.

Oftentimes, we find ourselves in spiritual battle. In His mercy, God sends us special help through our heavenly Mother, the Virgin Mary, and special friends such as Saint Michael the Archangel.

Whenever you find yourself in the midst of a spiritual battle, do not forget that the Rosary is an invincible weapon because Mary is the realization of God's promise that a woman would crush the serpent's head (see Gn 3:15).

You can also count on Saint Michael's help; his heavenly army has assured victory over the fallen angels (see Rv 12:7–8). You can ask for his help:

> Saint Michael the Archangel, defend us in battle;
> be our safeguard against the wickedness and snares of the devil.
> May God rebuke him, we humbly pray:
> and you, O Prince of the heavenly hosts,
> by the power of God,
> cast down to hell Satan and the other evil spirits,
> who prowl through the world for the ruin of souls. Amen.
> (*Prayers against the Powers of Darkness* 42)

As you complete your reflection and prayer today, let these words from Psalm 116 fill your heart with thanksgiving.

> *⁷Return, my soul, to your rest;*
> *the LORD has been very good to you.*
> *⁸For my soul has been freed from death,*
> *my eyes from tears, my feet from stumbling.*
> (Ps 116:7–8, *NAB*)

What is the fruit of your reflection today?

_____
_____
_____
_____
_____

Day 4

When praying for healing, it is important to have faith. In other words, pray with faith.

Let us start today with a passage from the Gospel of Matthew, to remind our souls that we can approach Jesus with trust.

> [7]*Ask, and it will be given you; search, and you will find; knock, and the door will be opened for you.* [8]*For everyone who asks receives, and everyone who searches finds, and for everyone who knocks, the door will be opened.* [9]*Is there anyone among you who, if your child asks for bread, will give a stone?* [10]*Or if the child asks for a fish, will give a snake?* [11]*If you then, who are evil, know how to give good gifts to your children, how much more will your Father in heaven give good things to those who ask him!* (Mt 7:7–11)

Today, I invite you to let Jesus heal your self-image.

Through the years, you might have listened to lies the world and other people have told about you. Maybe you have believed them and built a false self-image based on these lies.

When you have a false self-image, you believe things such as "I'm not _____ (good, smart, attractive, strong . . .) enough" when they are not true.

To be healed, it is necessary to listen to the truth that is in the Word of God.

> [31]*Then Jesus said to the Jews who had believed in him, "If you continue in my word, you are truly my disciples;* [32]*and you will know the truth, and the truth will make you free."* (Jn 8:31–32)

In this reflection, it is important to learn and differentiate between the things you *do* that need to change, such as your sinful ways and bad choices, and the person you really *are* at the core of your soul.

The Word of God tells you that you were created out of love in God's image and likeness. Your soul reflects the goodness and beauty of the Lord. This is the plain truth about you.

Listen to the scriptures and believe what God has to say about you. Read the following passages and let the Word of God convince your soul of who you are in God's eyes.

> *[14] But Zion said, "The LORD has forsaken me;*
> *my Lord has forgotten me."*
> *[15] Can a mother forget her infant,*
> *be without tenderness for the child of her womb?*
> *Even should she forget,*
> *I will never forget you.* (Is 49:14–15, *NAB*)

> *[20] Is Ephraim not my favored son,*
> *the child in whom I delight?*
> *Even though I threaten him,*
> *I must still remember him!*
> *My heart stirs for him,*
> *I must show him compassion!—oracle of the LORD.*
> (Jer 31:20, *NAB*)

> *[16b] Do not fear, Zion,*
> *do not be discouraged!*
> *[17] The LORD, your God, is in your midst,*
> *a mighty savior,*
> *Who will rejoice over you with gladness,*
> *and renew you in his love,*
> *Who will sing joyfully because of you.* (Zep 3:16b–17, *NAB*)

> *[10] My beloved spoke and said to me,*
> > *"Arise, my darling,*
> > *my beautiful one, come with me.*

11 See! The winter is past;
   the rains are over and gone.
12 Flowers appear on the earth;
   the season of singing has come,
the cooing of doves
   is heard in our land.
13 The fig tree forms its early fruit;
   the blossoming vines spread their fragrance.
Arise, come, my darling;
   my beautiful one, come with me."

14 My dove in the clefts of the rock,
   in the hiding places on the mountainside,
show me your face,
   let me hear your voice;
for your voice is sweet,
   and your face is lovely. (Sg 2:10–14, *NIV*)

Read the passages above again, this time listening as God addresses you by your own name, rather than Zion and Ephraim.

Write down your reactions to what you just read of the Word of God. What truth are these words telling you?

_____
_____
_____
_____
_____

Let us pray:

> Dear God, I come to You today to ask You to heal my self-image. Give me the grace of being transformed by Your Word and able to believe the truth about myself. Touch my soul that I might be free from all falsehoods spoken about

me. You know me better than anybody else, and You love me as I am. Let me grow in self-knowledge so I can humbly appreciate the good that is in me. I praise You for creating me and for helping me become the person that I am, and I offer up to You all that is good in me. Dear God, heal me and let me flourish in Your image and likeness. Amen.

Complete this prayer with these verses from Psalm 139. Keep these words close to your heart throughout the day as you take care of your chores.

> *¹³You formed my inmost being;*
> *you knit me in my mother's womb.*
> *¹⁴I praise you, because I am wonderfully made;*
> *wonderful are your works!* (Ps 139:13–14, *NAB*)

Thank You, Lord, for who You made me to be!

What is the fruit of your reflection today?

_____
_____
_____
_____
_____

Day 5

The Lord, more than anyone else, wants you to be free from all your distresses.

He wants to free you from your emotional afflictions, fears, traumas, and painful memories. The Lord wants to heal you of all emotional pain so you can live life to the fullest. Jesus came so that you "may have life, and have it abundantly" (Jn 10:10).

Jesus died on the cross so that you might have life in abundance. Jesus suffered all sorts of pain so that you no longer needed to suffer. Jesus knows about your emotional pain because in his passion, He suffered anguish, affliction, and loneliness. He suffered it all for you. Thanks to His suffering, you can be healed of your emotional distress.

> *[4] Yet it was our pain that he bore,*
> *our sufferings he endured.*
> *We thought of him as stricken,*
> *struck down by God and afflicted.*
> *[5] But he was pierced for our sins,*
> *crushed for our iniquity.*
> *He bore the punishment that makes us whole,*
> *by his wounds we were healed.* (Is 53:4–5, *NAB*)

Write in the space bellow, "By His wounds, I am healed," and take a moment to ponder the sentence.

_____

_____

Today, let us pray for emotional healing.

Most emotional pains are wounds in our inner selves. Their roots can be traced to things that were done to us; things we did to ourselves or to others, deliberately or in ignorance; circumstances of life that are difficult to accept, or patterns of behaviors that have been passed down through generations.

Jesus can heal your wounds, whatever their roots may be, because He can reach the roots and take them away by the power of the blood He shed upon the cross. You can turn over your emotional hurts to Jesus. Lay them at the foot of the cross. He receives your heavy and afflicted heart, your fears, your worries, your hopelessness, your sadness, and your loneliness.

There is no emotional pain that Jesus will not receive. Listen to what He says to you.

> *^{28}Come to me, all you that are weary and are carrying heavy burdens, and I will give you rest. ^{29}Take my yoke upon you, and learn from me; for I am gentle and humble in heart, and you will find rest for your souls. ^{30}For my yoke is easy, and my burden is light. (Mt 11:28–30)*

> *^{6}Do not worry about anything, but in everything by prayer and supplication with thanksgiving let your requests be made known to God. 7 And the peace of God, which surpasses all understanding, will guard your hearts and your minds in Christ Jesus. (Phil 4:6–7)*

> *^{7}Cast all your anxiety on him, because he cares for you. (1 Pt 5:7)*

With great confidence that Jesus cares about you, tell Him about your afflictions.

> Dear Jesus, You know me deeply, and nothing within me is hidden from You. You know all my inner wounds and their roots. You love me, and You want me healed and whole because You care about me deeply. You have the power and authority to heal because You are God and You came to this earth to heal and save me. I am hurting, and I come to You in faith with my wounds, and I humbly pray for heal-

ing. Please touch the roots of my wounds and heal me so I can love You with all my heart and soul. Amen.

Continue your prayer with your own words, asking Jesus to visit your heart and bring healing to your emotional distress. Write down your prayer and be specific about the wounds you are asking to be healed.

_____
_____
_____
_____
_____

When you've finished writing your prayer, close your eyes and stay still for a few moments. Let Jesus look at you with His loving gaze. Let His love penetrate your soul, healing and bringing peace.

Finally, read this passage from Ben Sira and let it soak into your soul.

> *[19]The eyes of the Lord are upon those who love him;*
> *he is their mighty shield and strong support,*
> *A shelter from the heat, a shade from the noonday sun,*
> *a guard against stumbling, a help against falling.*
> *[20]He lifts up spirits, brings a sparkle to the eyes,*
> *gives health and life and blessing.* (Sir 34:19–20, *NAB*)

What is the fruit of your reflection today?

_____
_____
_____
_____
_____

Day 6

Today, let us pray for physical healing.

To prepare your heart, ponder over these passages from the Gospels. The first is a bit long, but you will find it very appropriate for your reflection today.

> ^{21}*When Jesus had again crossed over by boat to the other side of the lake, a large crowd gathered around him while he was by the lake.* ^{22}*Then one of the synagogue leaders, named Jairus, came, and when he saw Jesus, he fell at his feet.* ^{23}*He pleaded earnestly with him, "My little daughter is dying. Please come and put your hands on her so that she will be healed and live."* ^{24}*So Jesus went with him.*
>
> *A large crowd followed and pressed around him.* ^{25}*And a woman was there who had been subject to bleeding for twelve years.* ^{26}*She had suffered a great deal under the care of many doctors and had spent all she had, yet instead of getting better she grew worse.* ^{27}*When she heard about Jesus, she came up behind him in the crowd and touched his cloak,* ^{28}*because she thought, "If I just touch his clothes, I will be healed."* ^{29}*Immediately her bleeding stopped and she felt in her body that she was freed from her suffering.* ^{30}*At once Jesus realized that power had gone out from him. He turned around in the crowd and asked, "Who touched my clothes?"* ^{31}*"You see the people crowding against you," his disciples answered, "and yet you can ask, 'Who touched me?'"* ^{32}*But Jesus kept looking around to see who had done it.* ^{33}*Then the woman, knowing what had happened to her, came and fell at his feet and, trembling with fear, told him the whole truth.* ^{34}*He said to her, "Daughter, your faith has healed you. Go in peace and be freed from your suffering."*

> *³⁵While Jesus was still speaking, some people came from the house of Jairus, the synagogue leader. "Your daughter is dead," they said. "Why bother the teacher anymore?" ³⁶Overhearing what they said, Jesus told him, "Don't be afraid; just believe." ³⁷He did not let anyone follow him except Peter, James and John the brother of James. ³⁸When they came to the home of the synagogue leader, Jesus saw a commotion, with people crying and wailing loudly. ³⁹He went in and said to them, "Why all this commotion and wailing? The child is not dead but asleep." ⁴⁰But they laughed at him. After he put them all out, he took the child's father and mother and the disciples who were with him, and went in where the child was. ⁴¹He took her by the hand and said to her, "Talitha koum!" (which means "Little girl, I say to you, get up!"). ⁴²Immediately the girl stood up and began to walk around (she was twelve years old). At this they were completely astonished. ⁴³He gave strict orders not to let anyone know about this, and told them to give her something to eat.* (Mk 5:21–43, *NIV*)

This passage tells of two healings performed for serious conditions that the medicine of the time was not able to help. They confirm Jesus's mission as our savior and healer. And they show His compassion in the face of human suffering.

In both healings, there is an essential component of faith, from the sick woman and from the father of the child.

Read again verses 27 and 28. Write down what the woman said to herself and ponder these words.

_____

_____

With the faith you have, be it small or big, pray today with your own words, presenting to God your needs for physical healing.

_____

_____

_____

The second passage for your reflection today is from Matthew.

> ⁵When Jesus had entered Capernaum, a centurion came to him, asking for help. ⁶"Lord," he said, "my servant lies at home paralyzed, suffering terribly." ⁷Jesus said to him, "Shall I come and heal him?" ⁸The centurion replied, "Lord, I do not deserve to have you come under my roof. But just say the word, and my servant will be healed. ⁹For I myself am a man under authority, with soldiers under me. I tell this one, 'Go,' and he goes; and that one, 'Come,' and he comes. I say to my servant, 'Do this,' and he does it." ¹⁰When Jesus heard this, he was amazed and said to those following him, "Truly I tell you, I have not found anyone in Israel with such great faith. ¹¹I say to you that many will come from the east and the west, and will take their places at the feast with Abraham, Isaac and Jacob in the kingdom of heaven. ¹²But the subjects of the kingdom will be thrown outside, into the darkness, where there will be weeping and gnashing of teeth." ¹³Then Jesus said to the centurion, "Go! Let it be done just as you believed it would." And his servant was healed at that moment.
>
> ¹⁴When Jesus came into Peter's house, he saw Peter's mother-in-law lying in bed with a fever. ¹⁵He touched her hand and the fever left her, and she got up and began to wait on him. (Mt 8:5–15, NIV)

What stands out to you in this reading?

In the same way that the centurion asked Jesus to heal his servant, you also can present to God the needs of people you know who are suffering with illnesses.

Write down your prayer.

_____
_____
_____
_____
_____

> Thank You, Jesus, for You hear my prayer. I trust You to answer all my prayers according to Your wisdom and compassion. Amen.

What is the fruit of your reflection today?

_____
_____
_____
_____
_____

Day 7

The Lord not only heals us but uses us as healing tools for our brothers and sisters.

On many occasions, Jesus invited His disciples to participate in His mission. Read the following passages to learn about this.

> *¹Then Jesus called the twelve together and gave them power and authority over all demons and to cure diseases, ²and he sent them out to proclaim the kingdom of God and to heal.* (Lk 9:1–2)

> *⁷As you go, proclaim the good news, 'The kingdom of heaven has come near.' ⁸ᵃCure the sick, raise the dead, cleanse the lepers, cast out demons.* (Mt 10:7–8a)

> *¹²Very truly, I tell you, the one who believes in me will also do the works that I do and, in fact, will do greater works than these, because I am going to the Father. ¹³I will do whatever you ask in my name, so that the Father may be glorified in the Son. ¹⁴If in my name you ask me for anything, I will do it.* (Jn 14:12–14)

The disciples understood what Jesus was asking them to do. After Jesus ascended into heaven, the Christians of the early Church carried on His mission as reported in the Acts of the Apostles.

> *¹One day Peter and John were going up to the temple at the hour of prayer, at three o'clock in the afternoon. ²And a man lame from birth was being carried in. People would lay him daily at the gate of the temple called the Beautiful Gate so that he could ask for alms from those entering the temple. ³When he saw Peter and John about to go into the temple, he asked them for alms. ⁴Peter looked intently at him, as did John, and said, "Look at us." ⁵And he fixed his attention on*

them, expecting to receive something from them. ⁶But Peter said, "I have no silver or gold, but what I have I give you; in the name of Jesus Christ of Nazareth, stand up and walk." ⁷And he took him by the right hand and raised him up; and immediately his feet and ankles were made strong. ⁸Jumping up, he stood and began to walk, and he entered the temple with them, walking and leaping and praising God. ⁹All the people saw him walking and praising God, ¹⁰and they recognized him as the one who used to sit and ask for alms at the Beautiful Gate of the temple; and they were filled with wonder and amazement at what had happened to him. (Acts 3:1–10)

¹²Now many signs and wonders were done among the people through the apostles. And they were all together in Solomon's Portico. ¹³None of the rest dared to join them, but the people held them in high esteem. ¹⁴Yet more than ever believers were added to the Lord, great numbers of both men and women, ¹⁵so that they even carried out the sick into the streets, and laid them on cots and mats, in order that Peter's shadow might fall on some of them as he came by. ¹⁶A great number of people would also gather from the towns around Jerusalem, bringing the sick and those tormented by unclean spirits, and they were all cured. (Acts 5:12–16)

Ponder this: "and they were all cured." How amazing is our Lord!

Today, I urge you to consider how you can participate in Jesus's mission and bring healing to others.

As you saw in today's readings, Jesus wants to share His mission with us. How many around you are in need of spiritual, emotional, or physical healing? How can you help? Listen to God speaking within your heart and write down your reflections about this.

_____
_____
_____
_____
_____

Take a moment today to pray for those who are suffering right now. With your own words, write down your prayer for them.

_____
_____
_____
_____
_____

This week, you have reflected on and prayed about the different ways God heals His children. What were your main reflections about healing? How did God heal you this week? Review your reflections from the week and write below what you learned that is new, surprising, or transformative.

_____
_____
_____
_____
_____
_____
_____
_____
_____
_____

Week 4

Prayer

*Persevere in prayer, being watchful in it with thanksgiving;
at the same time, pray for us too.*
(Col 4:2–3a, *NAB*)

Day 1

This week, we will continue on our path of reflection and prayer with the Word of God, meditating on prayer itself.

Let us start by considering how Jesus prayed. Read the following passages and consider what you can learn from His example.

> ^{12}Now during those days he went out to the mountain to pray; and he spent the night in prayer to God. (Lk 6:12)

> ^{35}In the morning, while it was still very dark, he got up and went out to a deserted place, and there he prayed. (Mk 1:35)

> ^{22}Immediately he made the disciples get into the boat and go on ahead to the other side, while he dismissed the crowds. ^{23}And after he had dismissed the crowds, he went up the mountain by himself to pray. When evening came, he was there alone. (Mt 14:22–23)

In His moments of prayer, Jesus would go to an isolated place to encounter His Father alone. He would talk to His Father about whatever was going on in His life.

With the verses below, notice that Jesus prayed in moments of joy as well as in moments of anguish. He also prayed to intercede for others. He would simply open His heart to His Father in a sincere dialogue.

> ^{21}At that same hour Jesus rejoiced in the Holy Spirit and said, "I thank you, Father, Lord of heaven and earth, because you have hidden these things from the wise and the intelligent and have revealed them to infants; yes, Father, for such was your gracious will." (Lk 10:21)

> ^{36}He said, "Abba, Father, for you all things are possible; remove this cup from me; yet, not what I want, but what you want." (Mk 14:36)

> ^{31}Simon, Simon, listen! Satan has demanded to sift all of you like wheat, ^{32}but I have prayed for you that your own faith may not fail; and you, when once you have turned back, strengthen your brothers. (Lk 22:31–32)

Prayer makes more sense when you just open your heart and talk to God as you would to a friend who listens and understands you completely. In prayer, you can approach Jesus and talk to Him about whatever is going on in your life with complete trust.

The very first thing you are called to do to grow in your private prayer is to develop the habit of spending time alone with God.

When you pray, put yourself in the presence of God. Look at Him within yourself, in the innermost and quietest place of your soul. Look at Him with eyes of faith and praise Him. Then look at yourself and take note of how you are in the moment. Present yourself to Him as you are, offering up your praise and thanksgiving, your sins, your needs, your worries, your very self.

> ^{6}But whenever you pray, go into your room and shut the door and pray to your Father who is in secret; and your Father who sees in secret will reward you. (Mt 6:6)

Take a moment to experience being in the presence of God. Open your heart with faith, sincerity, and humility, and tell Him what is going on with you right now.

Start praying:

> Dear Lord, I come before You with a humble and open heart. I praise You and give You thanks for this very moment. Thank You for the gift of prayer. It is Your Holy Spirit that touches me right now and brings me to Your presence.

Close your eyes and stay still for a few moments, pondering the presence of God within you.

> I offer up to You my thanksgiving for all the wonderful things in my life. Thank You for my life, for the ones I love, and for all You do for us. I also offer up to You my weaknesses and limitations [name them], my needs [name them], my worries and concerns [name them], and my crosses and sacrifices [name them]. Thank You for taking care of me and the ones I love. I ask You to expand this moment of prayer so I can live this whole day in Your presence. Amen.

Continue praying as your soul leads you.

When you are done, write down a summary of your thoughts and feelings during this prayer.

_____
_____
_____
_____
_____

Prayer is a path that requires practice and learning. I encourage you to develop the habit of having daily meetings with God, reserving a set time and place for them.

It helps if you make a commitment to meet with God in a certain time and place everyday, even though you may sometimes need to be flexible. Consider your daily schedule to determine the duration of your prayer. Some people can give thirty minutes or more to God every day in a quiet room or chapel; others can only offer ten minutes or so during the morning commute to work, or during baby's nap time, or while on the treadmill at the gym. All of these are good; whatever fits your schedule.

Week 4

Take a moment to think about a good place, time, and duration for your daily prayer. Write down your commitment below.

_____
_____
_____
_____
_____

Think about what has stood out for you about prayer. Write it down in one sentence.

_____
_____
_____
_____
_____

What is the fruit of your reflection today?

_____
_____
_____
_____
_____

Day 2

Prayer is a search for transformation in Christ, a response to our innermost desire to be in Christ.

Once you have made a commitment to meet with Jesus on a daily basis, you will grow in your friendship with Him. In other words, prayer is more than just an activity we add to our daily routine. It is a path, a journey, that leads to continued growth in closeness to and participation in God's love.

As with every path, the first step is one we might not be sure how to take. The disciples saw Jesus praying and wondered. They wanted to pray, but they did not know how, so they asked Jesus to teach them.

> *¹He was praying in a certain place, and when he had finished, one of his disciples said to him, "Lord, teach us to pray just as John taught his disciples."* (Lk 11:1)

This is the prayer Jesus taught them, which has been handed down to us as the Lord's Prayer:

> Our Father who art in heaven,
> hallowed be thy name.
> Thy kingdom come.
> Thy will be done on earth, as it is in heaven.
> Give us this day our daily bread,
> and forgive us our trespasses,
> as we forgive those who trespass against us,
> and lead us not into temptation,
> but deliver us from evil.
> (*Catechism of the Catholic Church*)

As an exercise of prayer, read the Lord's Prayer a second time. This time ponder each line.

Pick a line that speaks to you and write it down.

_____
_____

Repeat this line many times in your heart, letting it soak into your soul. In the presence of God, rest with this line.

Then, ask yourself: What is God telling me with this line? How can I apply it to my life today?

_____
_____
_____
_____
_____

Prayer is a dialogue. What is your response to what God is telling you?

_____
_____
_____
_____
_____

What is the fruit of your reflection today?

_____
_____
_____
_____

Day 3

Today, I invite you to ponder over how to pray.

When we talk about how to pray, it is normal to think about types of prayer (praise, thanksgiving, petition, intercession, etc.) or formats of prayer (Rosary, novenas, written prayers, spontaneous prayers, meditation, etc.).

However, today's reflection goes beyond types and formats of prayer. In this reflection, "how to pray" refers to the inner disposition of the heart, no matter what kind of prayer. According to the Word of God, one inner disposition that is important for praying is faith.

> *^{22}Whatever you ask for in prayer with faith, you will receive.*
> (Mt 21:22)

Consider the parable below and think about faith and perseverance.

> *^{1}Then Jesus told them a parable about their need to pray always and not to lose heart. ^{2}He said, "In a certain city there was a judge who neither feared God nor had respect for people. ^{3}In that city there was a widow who kept coming to him and saying, 'Grant me justice against my opponent.' ^{4}For a while he refused; but later he said to himself, 'Though I have no fear of God and no respect for anyone, ^{5}yet because this widow keeps bothering me, I will grant her justice, so that she may not wear me out by continually coming.'" ^{6}And the Lord said, "Listen to what the unjust judge says. ^{7}And will not God grant justice to his chosen ones who cry to him day and night? Will he delay long in helping them? ^{8}I tell you, he will quickly grant justice to them. And yet, when the Son of Man comes, will he find faith on earth?"*
> (Lk 18:1–8)

Write down the verse that stands out to you.

_____

_____

Let this verse inspire you to pray in the same way you did with yesterday's prayer exercise. Ponder the verse you picked. There's no need to rush. Then listen with your heart to what God is telling you through this verse. Stay a few moments with this thought as it fills your heart. Finally, write down your response to God.

_____

_____

_____

_____

_____

You probably want to grow in prayer but face many difficulties and find yourself in need of more faith and perseverance. You can't do it by yourself; you need the assistance of the Holy Spirit, who will give you all the grace you need for your spiritual growth.

> [26] *Likewise the Spirit helps us in our weakness; for we do not know how to pray as we ought, but that very Spirit intercedes with sighs too deep for words.* [27] *And God, who searches the heart, knows what is the mind of the Spirit, because the Spirit intercedes for the saints according to the will of God.* (Rom 8:26–27)

Let us pray and ask for the gift of prayer.

> Dear God, I don't know how to pray as I ought. I don't have enough faith. I beg You, dear God, strengthen my faith. I do not persevere in my prayers. I pray for a few days, and then I become lukewarm and let other things take the place of my moment of prayer. O God, look at my weakness and have mercy. Send Your Holy Spirit to aid me.

Without the Holy Spirit, I cannot even say Your sweet name, my dear Jesus. I need Your help. I trust in You. Give me grace, and I will grow in my prayer life. Give me grace, and my soul will rejoice in friendship with You. I open up my heart to receive Your grace. Amen.

What is the fruit of your reflection today?

_____
_____
_____
_____
_____

Day 4

Let us continue our reflection on how to pray. Yesterday, we reflected on the need to pray with faith and perseverance. Today, I invite you to reflect on humility.

> *^{21}The prayer of the lowly pierces the clouds;*
> *it does not rest till it reaches its goal;*
> *Nor will it withdraw till the Most High responds.* (Sir 35:21, NAB)

Consider the parable below as you reflect on humility in prayer.

> *^{9}He also told this parable to some who trusted in themselves that they were righteous and regarded others with contempt: ^{10}"Two men went up to the temple to pray, one a Pharisee and the other a tax collector. ^{11}The Pharisee, standing by himself, was praying thus, 'God, I thank you that I am not like other people: thieves, rogues, adulterers, or even like this tax collector. ^{12}I fast twice a week; I give a tenth of all my income.' ^{13}But the tax collector, standing far off, would not even look up to heaven, but was beating his breast and saying, 'God, be merciful to me, a sinner!' ^{14}I tell you, this man went down to his home justified rather than the other; for all who exalt themselves will be humbled, but all who humble themselves will be exalted."* (Lk 18:9–14)

Read the parable a second time, slowly, taking your time and pondering each verse. Pick a verse that calls your attention and write it down.

_____

_____

_____

Put yourself in the presence of God and meditate on this verse. What is God telling you with this verse?

_____
_____
_____
_____
_____

What is your response to what God is telling you?

_____
_____
_____
_____
_____

What is the fruit of your meditation?

_____
_____
_____
_____
_____

Now go back and look at what you have done today and observe the steps you have taken to complete your meditation.

Is this process one you can continue doing in your daily prayer? Think about it. This is how Mary prayed.

> [19] *And Mary kept all these things, reflecting on them in her heart.*
> (Lk 2:19, *NAB*)

What is the fruit of your reflection today?

Day 5

Over the last two days, you have reflected on the inner dispositions necessary to praying well, such as faith and humility. Let us continue this reflection by looking at Jesus's example.

How did Jesus pray? What was His most notable inner disposition?

Jesus prayed with a completely surrendered heart. He asked the Father that He might be saved from death, but He embraced His Father's will. His prayer was heard and answered in a more perfect way.

Out of love, Jesus was not saved from the cross, but through the cross, He was granted a greater answer—that is, resurrection and eternal salvation for all humankind.

> *[7]In the days of his flesh, Jesus offered up prayers and supplications, with loud cries and tears, to the one who was able to save him from death, and he was heard because of his reverent submission. [8]Although he was a Son, he learned obedience through what he suffered; [9]and having been made perfect, he became the source of eternal salvation for all who obey him, [10]having been designated by God a high priest according to the order of Melchizedek.* (Heb 5:7–10)

To follow Jesus's steps in prayer is to be prepared to offer up our crosses and sacrifices.

In faith and humility, we believe all prayers are heard, while we surrender our will to God's wisdom and love.

According to the Word of God, Jesus was humble to the point of being completely detached from His human will, to fully embrace the will of the Father.

> *⁵Have among yourselves the same attitude that is also yours in Christ Jesus,*
> *⁶Who, though he was in the form of God,*
> *did not regard equality with God something to be grasped.*
> *⁷Rather, he emptied himself,*
> *taking the form of a slave,*
> *coming in human likeness;*
> *and found human in appearance,*
> *⁸he humbled himself,*
> *becoming obedient to death, even death on a cross.*
> *⁹Because of this, God greatly exalted him*
> *and bestowed on him the name*
> *that is above every name*
> *¹⁰that at the name of Jesus*
> *every knee should bend,*
> *of those in heaven and on earth and under the earth,*
> *¹¹and every tongue confess that*
> *Jesus Christ is Lord,*
> *to the glory of God the Father.* (Phil 2:5–11, *NAB*)

Because of His humble obedience and detachment, Jesus is our path to God. In other words, Jesus is our prayer. It is through Him, with Him, and in Him that we pray and find our way to God. So we pray, "Jesus, make our hearts as humble and obedient as Yours."

I invite you to complete your prayer following these steps:

1. Put yourself in the presence of God and take time to wonder about the greatness of God that dwells within you.
2. Present yourself humbly before God as you are right now, offering up whatever you have (your sins, your thanksgiving, your petitions, your crosses, your will, your very self).
3. Read again the passages above, slowly, absorbing each verse.
4. Pick a verse that calls your attention and stay with it, letting it talk to you.
5. Respond to God with a prayer and consider how to apply your response to your life.

6. Finally, write down what stands out to you as you've prayed.

___

What is the fruit of your reflection today?

___

Day 6

Prayer is dialogue with God. You talk to Him, and He talks to you.

You talk to Him, offering your praise, thanksgiving, petitions, intercessions, and your daily sacrifices—whether the little ones you choose ("Lord, I offer up to You this piece of candy that I choose not to eat today") or the ones He allows to happen to you ("Lord, it is frustrating to have such a difficult boss, but I offer up to You my frustration").

The Word of God encourages you to talk to God in many ways.

Read the verses below to see references the Word of God makes to praise, petition, and intercession.

> ^{2}*I will praise you, LORD, with all my heart;*
> *I will declare all your wondrous deeds.*
> ^{3}*I will delight and rejoice in you;*
> *I will sing hymns to your name, Most High.* (Ps 9:2–3, NAB)

> ^{24}*Until now you have not asked for anything in my name. Ask and you will receive, so that your joy may be complete.* (Jn 16:24)

> ^{18}*Pray in the Spirit at all times in every prayer and supplication. To that end keep alert and always persevere in supplication for all the saints.* (Eph 6:18)

Since it is a dialogue, God also talks to you.

He may talk to you during your private prayer through the Bible, through a reading from a devotional book or the life of a saint, or through a thought. Sometimes, He chooses to talk after your prayer, during the day, through a happening or a word from someone else.

It is a good idea to have a journal to write down all these little pearls; in many situations, they are pieces of a puzzle to be put together over time.

God is very creative in His communication. To Moses, He spoke through a burning bush (see Ex 3:1–5); to Peter, through a vision (see Acts 10:9–23); and to Joseph, through a dream (see Matthew 1:20).

However, most of the time, He speaks through a "gentle whisper" (see 1 Kgs 19:11–12, *NIV*). It is necessary to open your heart to listen to God as He speaks to you in the silence of your heart. Say, along with young Samuel, "Speak, LORD, for your servant is listening" (see 1 Sm 3:10, *NAB*).

Sometimes, the dialogue does not consist of words as God talks in the silence. This dialogue is more like an exchange of presence.

God is present in you, and you are present in God. You look at Him, and He looks at you.

Sometimes, you are called just to be in the presence of God. This dialogue can be more profound because it goes beyond words. Sometimes, we simply need to stop talking and just be quiet and listen.

Have you ever enjoyed the sun in the springtime? You just appreciate the warmth, and that is enough. Or have you ever been company to a loved one going through a painful loss? Words are useless. A touch, a gentle hug, a silent company is all that is needed.

I invite you to try a new exercise of prayer, a new type of dialogue. Read the following passage.

> *32They went to a place called Gethsemane; and he said to his disciples, "Sit here while I pray." 33He took with him Peter and James and John, and began to be distressed and agitated. 34And he said to them, "I am deeply grieved, even to death; remain here, and keep awake." 35And going a little farther, he threw himself on the ground and prayed that, if it were possible, the hour might pass from him. 36He said, "Abba, Father, for you all things are possible; remove this cup from*

> me; yet, not what I want, but what you want." ³⁷He came and found them sleeping; and he said to Peter, "Simon, are you asleep? Could you not keep awake one hour? ³⁸Keep awake and pray that you may not come into the time of trial; the spirit indeed is willing, but the flesh is weak." ³⁹And again he went away and prayed, saying the same words. ⁴⁰And once more he came and found them sleeping, for their eyes were very heavy; and they did not know what to say to him. ⁴¹He came a third time and said to them, "Are you still sleeping and taking your rest? Enough! The hour has come; the Son of Man is betrayed into the hands of sinners. ⁴²Get up, let us be going. See, my betrayer is at hand." (Mk 14:32–42)

Now, read the passage again and imagine yourself being present with Jesus. Imagine the scene: darkness beneath the olive trees, Jesus fallen upon the ground in anguish. Look at Jesus in His painful moment and approach Him. No words are necessary, just a silent, loving company. Stay still and just keep Him company. He looks at you, and you can see the pain in His eyes. Imagine how Jesus receives your consoling presence by His side. Stay as long as you wish in this moment of prayer.

When done, write down your experience.

_____
_____
_____
_____

What is the fruit of your reflection today?

_____
_____
_____
_____

Day 7

This week, you have reflected on and prayed about prayer. I have presented to you a path for growth based on the example of Jesus and what the Word of God tells us about prayer. You have learned and practiced steps for meditation, and you have considered prayer as a dialogue that takes many forms.

Now, it is important to note that the steps I presented for meditation are only one path among many. I hope they work well for you, but don't be afraid to explore other ways that might fit you better. Some people prefer to spend their moment of private prayer meditating on the Rosary with the Virgin Mary. Others like to talk to their favorite saints, pray novenas, read a devotional book, or sing songs with uplifting lyrics.

What you actually do in your moment of private prayer is less important than the disposition of your heart and the inner sense of being in the presence of God.

Nevertheless, there are two things I invite you to ponder today. First, whatever kind of prayer suits you, do not give up praying. I invite you to make a commitment of daily prayer, and I encourage you to be faithful to this commitment. There will be days when you feel lazy, tired, busy, sick, distracted, or worried. Do not let any of these things take you away from prayer.

Pray as you are, even if the only thing you can do is repeat the name of Jesus. If you can, tell Him how you feel and talk about your struggles. If praying is difficult, ask for help. Ask the Holy Spirit to aid you. Ask the Virgin Mary and the saints to pray with you. Ask your guardian angel to remind you to pray and be faithful. If you persevere, you will see the fruits.

Second, prayer is a process, like that of planting a seed, caring for the plant, watching the flowers bloom, and awaiting the ripening of its fruits while new fruits are already blossoming. No matter the manner of your prayer, you will know you are praying as you ought if your prayer bears fruits.

And what are the fruits of prayer? You'll know your prayer is fruitful when, after some time of daily and faithful prayer, you notice that Jesus has become more central in your life and your love for Jesus has increased.

The most essential purpose of prayer is to make you fall in love with Jesus. Because He loved you first.

> [11]*Beloved, since God loved us so much, we also ought to love one another.* [12]*No one has ever seen God; if we love one another, God lives in us, and his love is perfected in us.* (1 Jn 4:11–12)

In conclusion, prayer has achieved its purpose when our lives are transformed in love.

Read the following passage and meditate with it, following the steps of meditation that you have learned this week.

> [4]*Love is patient; love is kind; love is not envious or boastful or arrogant* [5]*or rude. It does not insist on its own way; it is not irritable or resentful;* [6]*it does not rejoice in wrongdoing, but rejoices in the truth.* [7]*It bears all things, believes all things, hopes all things, endures all things.* (1 Cor 13:4–7)

This week, you have reflected on and prayed about prayer itself. You reflected about how to pray, and you experienced steps for meditation. Review your reflections, prayer exercises, and notes from the week and write below what you learned that is new, surprising, or transformative.

_____

_____

Week 5

Word of God

*Your word is a lamp for my feet,
a light for my path.*
(Ps 119:105, *NAB*)

Day 1

The book of Genesis starts with the revelation of God as the Creator of all that there is. In chapter 1, we find the expression "God said" eight times as creation unfolds and comes to the making of mankind (see Gn 1:1–27).

As "God said" the word, heavens, earth, light, waters, and all living creatures started to be. All creation came to be by the power of the Word of God. As the author of Hebrews says, "the universe was ordered by the word of God" (Heb 11:3, *NAB*). That is how powerful the Word of God is.

Psalm 33 praises the Lord who created the heavens and all the celestial creatures:

> ^{6}*By the* LORD*'s word the heavens were made;*
> *by the breath of his mouth all their host.* (Ps 33:6, *NAB*)

The simple thought that God created the universe with the power of His Word is enough to make our souls tremble in amazement. That is how the people of the Old Covenant felt.

However, that is not all. The apostle John, inspired by the Holy Spirit, rewrites Genesis in light of Christ and begins his Gospel with this powerful statement:

> ^{1}*In the beginning was the Word,*
> *and the Word was with God,*
> *and the Word was God.*
> ^{2}*He was in the beginning with God.*
> ^{3}*All things came to be through him,*
> *and without him nothing came to be.*

> *What came to be ⁴through him was life,*
> *and this life was the light of the human race;*
> *⁵the light shines in the darkness,*
> *and the darkness has not overcome it. . . .*
> *¹⁴And the Word became flesh*
> *and made his dwelling among us,*
> *and we saw his glory,*
> *the glory as of the Father's only Son,*
> *full of grace and truth.* (Jn 1:1–5, 14, *NAB*)

It becomes clear that the Word of God in Genesis is the Son. And that when the time was right, Jesus, the Word Incarnate, began a new creation, bringing a new kind of light to this world, a new kind of life to our souls.

Read again the passage above and meditate on it. I invite you, first, to be in a quiet awe before the powerful revelation of this text. Because it is the Word of God, it is powerful on its own. Let your soul be immersed in this Word that can create and transform anything.

Secondly, present yourself to Jesus and ask Him to recreate in your life the likeness of God, transforming your heart into a new heart. Let Jesus, through His Spirit, touch your understanding so you can grasp the revealed Truth and touch your heart so you can live the fullness of the Truth.

The Word of God that created all there is from nothing is powerful enough to recreate holiness out of our sinful lives. Ponder this and pray with your own words.

Write down your response to God based on your meditation.

_____
_____
_____
_____
_____

What is the fruit of your reflection today?

_____
_____
_____
_____
_____

Day 2

The whole Bible is the inspired Word of God. Every time you listen to or read the Bible, you are connecting with the true Word of God, which stands forever.

The sacred books of the Jews (the Law, Prophets, and Writings) are the written Word of God that comprises the Old Testament. The people of the Old Covenant revered the Word of God as eternal and truthful.

> *⁶A voice says, "Proclaim!"*
> *I answer, "What shall I proclaim?"*
> *"All flesh is grass,*
> *and all their loyalty like the flower of the field.*
> *⁷The grass withers, the flower wilts,*
> *when the breath of the LORD blows upon it."*
> *"Yes, the people is grass!*
> *⁸The grass withers, the flower wilts,*
> *but the word of our God stands forever."* (Is 40:6–8, NAB)

> *⁸⁹Your word, LORD, stands forever;*
> *it is firm as the heavens.*
> *⁹⁰Through all generations your truth endures;*
> *fixed to stand firm like the earth.* (Ps 119:89–90, NAB)

When Jesus, the Word made flesh, was teaching among us, He proclaimed the Kingdom of God and announced our salvation. Some of His words were difficult to understand and accept, even for His followers.

When Jesus was teaching about the Eucharist, many disciples were shocked by the words.

> *⁵⁶Whoever eats my flesh and drinks my blood remains in me and I in him.*
>
> *⁶⁶As a result of this, many [of] his disciples returned to their former way of life and no longer accompanied him. ⁶⁷Jesus then said to the Twelve, "Do you also want to leave?" ⁶⁸Simon Peter answered him, "Master, to whom shall we go? You have the words of eternal life. ⁶⁹We have come to believe and are convinced that you are the Holy One of God."* (Jn 6:56, 66–69, NAB)

Only Jesus, the Son of God, has the words of eternal life! Can you accept that Jesus is offered to you as the daily bread of the Eucharist and whispers in the deepest part of your soul, "Let there be eternal life"?

The Word that created the universe became flesh in Jesus Christ for our salvation and then was made bread so we could eat it and enter into friendship with God forever. Ponder this.

The next time you receive Communion, listen to the Word whispering within you.

What is the reaction of your heart to this reflection? How do you respond to God?

_____
_____
_____
_____
_____

After Jesus completed His mission and ascended into heaven, His apostles spread the words of eternal life to the world. Inspired by the Holy Spirit, the message was written for the sake of future generations. The Bible is then the written Word of God. It includes the books of the New Covenant in Jesus Christ that was added to the sacred books of the Old Covenant of the Jews.

To finish your reflection today, think about the reasons you seek growth in knowledge and intimacy with the Bible.

> *^{16}All scripture is inspired by God and is useful for teaching, for refutation, for correction, and for training in righteousness, ^{17}so that one who belongs to God may be competent, equipped for every good work.*
> (2 Tm 3:16–17, NAB)

With your own words, pray to God, asking for the grace to be closer to the Word of God.

Then consider, from a practical point of view, what you can do to grow in knowledge and intimacy with the Bible.

_____
_____
_____
_____
_____

What is the fruit of your reflection today?

_____
_____
_____
_____
_____

Day 3

How important it is to come closer to the sacred scriptures! As we learn and understand the will of God, we receive the grace to live according to it through our prayer and meditation.

Let us start today's reflection by praying with a passage from the Old Testament, and then let us meditate on a parable of the Gospel of Matthew.

> *[33] LORD, teach me the way of your statutes;*
> *I shall keep them with care.*
> *[34] Give me understanding to keep your law,*
> *to observe it with all my heart.*
> *[35] Lead me in the path of your commandments,*
> *for that is my delight.*
> *[36] Direct my heart toward your testimonies*
> *and away from gain.*
> *[37] Avert my eyes from what is worthless;*
> *by your way give me life.*
> *[38] For your servant, fulfill your promise*
> *made to those who fear you.*
> *[39] Turn away from me the taunts I dread,*
> *for your judgments are good.*
> *[40] See how I long for your precepts;*
> *in your righteousness give me life.* (Ps 119:33–40, NAB)

Ponder verse 40, letting your heart feel a longing for the Word of God.

The people of the Old Covenant understood the Word of God as the Law of Moses. Their desire was to be righteous in fulfilling the precepts and commandments of the Lord. It was part of the preparation for what was to come.

When the Father fulfilled His promise and Jesus revealed Himself as the Word Incarnate, the old law was perfected in love. In light of Christ, we now understand what it is our souls really long for, which is a loving relationship with Jesus.

Having a loving relationship with Jesus is our purpose in life. This is what God created us for.

Now, moving forward to a passage from the New Testament, meditate on the following text:

> *¹That same day Jesus went out of the house and sat beside the sea. ²Such great crowds gathered around him that he got into a boat and sat there, while the whole crowd stood on the beach. ³And he told them many things in parables, saying: "Listen! A sower went out to sow. ⁴And as he sowed, some seeds fell on the path, and the birds came and ate them up. ⁵Other seeds fell on rocky ground, where they did not have much soil, and they sprang up quickly, since they had no depth of soil. ⁶But when the sun rose, they were scorched; and since they had no root, they withered away. ⁷Other seeds fell among thorns, and the thorns grew up and choked them. ⁸Other seeds fell on good soil and brought forth grain, some a hundredfold, some sixty, some thirty."*
> (Mt 13:1–8)

Jesus explained the parable, saying to His disciples:

> *¹⁸Hear then the parable of the sower. ¹⁹When anyone hears the word of the kingdom and does not understand it, the evil one comes and snatches away what is sown in the heart; this is what was sown on the path. ²⁰As for what was sown on rocky ground, this is the one who hears the word and immediately receives it with joy; ²¹yet such a person has no root, but endures only for a while, and when trouble or persecution arises on account of the word, that person immediately falls away. ²²As for what was sown among thorns, this is the one who hears the word, but the cares of the world and the lure of wealth choke the*

word, and it yields nothing. ²³But as for what was sown on good soil, this is the one who hears the word and understands it, who indeed bears fruit and yields, in one case a hundredfold, in another sixty, and in another thirty. (Mt 13:18–23)

Talk to Jesus about this parable. Talk to Him as you would talk to a friend and share with Him your thoughts.

What is the seed? What kind of soil is your heart? What do you need to be a rich or richer soil? What is God inviting you to do through this parable?

_____

_____

_____

What is Jesus's response to your prayer?

_____

_____

_____

_____

Jesus, the Word of God, is the seed that wants to be planted within you to bear fruits of love in your life. Think about this.

To close your meditation today, go back to the first passage of this reflection and pray with Psalm 119:33–40 again. This time, use the expression "love of Jesus" instead of the words *statutes, law, commandments, precepts,* and *righteousness*.

What is the fruit of your reflection today?

_____

_____

_____

_____

Day 4

The Word of God itself invites us to spend time with it, studying, meditating, and reflecting on it.

> *33 If you are willing to listen, you can learn;*
> *if you pay attention, you can be instructed.*
>
> *34 Stand in the company of the elders;*
> *stay close to whoever is wise.*
> *35 Be eager to hear every discourse;*
> *let no insightful saying escape you.*
> *36 If you see the intelligent, seek them out;*
> *let your feet wear away their doorsteps!*
>
> *37 Reflect on the law of the Most High,*
> *and let his commandments be your constant study.*
> *Then he will enlighten your mind,*
> *and make you wise as you desire.* (Sir 6:33–37, *NAB*)
>
> *24 Listen to me, my son, and take my advice,*
> *and apply your mind to my words,*
> *25 While I pour out my spirit by measure*
> *and impart knowledge with care.* (Sir 16:24–25, *NAB*)

Many Catholics feel the desire to study and learn more about the Bible, but sometimes they feel intimidated by readings that are difficult to understand. If this is the case for you, do not give up but be diligent in searching, learning, and keeping the Word of God in your heart; in time, it will explain itself to you and fructify "in one case a hundredfold, in another sixty, and in another thirty" (see Mt 13:23).

Start by paying attention to the readings and homilies during Mass, and take some time to read the Bible every day. Make use of the footnotes that can be found in many Bibles, as they help explain some passages. You may also find good Catholic resources (books, videos, audios, talks, study groups) in your parish that will help you grow in your understanding of the Bible. All in all, keep the sacred scriptures close to you; the word of the Lord is sweeter than honey and pure as the fine gold (see Ps 19:11).

The *Catechism of the Catholic Church* (*CCC*) invites us to approach the Bible with faith and reason. Here are some tips for developing a habit of studying the Bible.

> According to an ancient tradition, one can distinguish between two senses of Scripture: the literal and the spiritual, the latter being subdivided into the allegorical, moral, and anagogical senses. (*CCC* 115)

The allegorical sense points to the meaning of the text in light of Christ. The moral sense instructs us in how to apply the Word to our lives. The anagogical points to eternal realities in heaven.

Let us try an exercise for applying the different senses of the Bible to a small excerpt.

The following reading from Isaiah tells us that the Word of God always fulfills its purpose.

> *[10]Yet just as from the heavens*
> *the rain and snow come down*
> *And do not return there*
> *till they have watered the earth,*
> *making it fertile and fruitful,*
> *Giving seed to the one who sows*
> *and bread to the one who eats,*
> *[11]So shall my word be*
> *that goes forth from my mouth;*
> *It shall not return to me empty,*

but shall do what pleases me,
achieving the end for which I sent it. (Is 55:10–11, *NAB*)

The literal sense refers to the face value of the text, to an understanding of the reading according to its literal words. In this case, the author of the reading above compared the Word of God to the rain and snow. He said that the rain is efficacious because it fulfills its purpose on the earth. It gives water to fertilize the soil so the seed can bear fruit and give bread to the hungry. The rain comes from above, as a gift, and does not go back in the form of vapor before it accomplishes its purpose of bringing fertility and bread to the earth.

In comparing the Word of God to the rain, what can you tell about the Word of God?

_____
_____
_____
_____
_____

Now, let us try to unfold some layers of the spiritual senses that go beyond the literal meaning of the text.

The allegorical sense points to Jesus. Consider that Jesus is the Word Incarnate who was sent for our salvation, which was accomplished through death on the cross and resurrection.

How is the passage above pointing to Jesus?

_____
_____
_____
_____
_____

Jesus achieved the end for which He was sent. Christ was sent by the Father, from above, as a gift of salvation for us. His coming was perfectly efficacious for our salvation. He died on the cross but did not stay dead and buried in the earth. Like the water of the rain, once His mission was accomplished, He returned to heaven in a resurrected body.

We can see in this text of Isaiah a prophecy about the Word Incarnate, whose plan of salvation has been accomplished.

Now, what can you tell about the moral sense? The moral sense leads to an invitation to respond to the Word.

Based on the text, how can you respond to God?

_____
_____
_____
_____
_____

Our basic response is a response of faith in Jesus, who accomplished a perfect salvation for us. We may consider approaching the Word of God with confidence, knowing that we can always find what we need because it always accomplishes its purpose. We may contemplate how the Bible has the answers for the deepest questions of the human heart and what leads us to desire a life guided by the Word of God. We may also want to meditate on Jesus, who pours His grace upon us, as the rain, and open our hearts to receive His gifts. Or we might meditate on the mystery of salvation, offering praises and thanksgiving to our Savior.

The anagogical sense illuminates our understanding of our destiny in eternity. How can you connect the text to realities beyond this earthly life and the glory of eternity in heaven?

_____
_____

_____

_____

_____

Consider that the final purpose of salvation is to bring us to participate in the divine life in heaven. By accepting Jesus into our hearts, we let His Word transform our souls into fertile and fruitful soil that makes the seed grow, such that one day, we will join the Trinity and dine on the heavenly bread in the presence of the Lord. That is the final end we expect to achieve, as we trust God will not abandon us empty-handed but will bring us to everlasting life. As the rain comes down and completes its job, we await the final coming of Jesus to renew the whole of creation for the complete fulfillment of the Word of God.

Review the literal and spiritual senses of the reading from Isaiah 55:10–11. Did this reflection on the Word of God bring growth to your knowledge and love of Jesus Christ? What is the fruit of this exercise? Is this something you would like to continue doing in order to grow in friendship with God?

_____

_____

_____

_____

_____

Finish your reflection with a prayer:

> Dear Jesus, Your words are sweeter than honey and pure as the purest gold. I want to taste Your sweetness and enrich my soul with Your grace. Give me the desire and the means to truly know Your word. Plant the seed of Your word inside me and touch my heart to make of it good soil. Send Your Holy Spirit to pour on me a rain of grace so Your word will grow within me and bear fruit through me.

Transform my life with the power of Your word and send me to speak the word for the transformation of others. Amen.

What is the fruit of your reflection today?

_____
_____
_____
_____
_____

Day 5

Today, I invite you to integrate study and prayer using the parables that Jesus taught us.

You will use the steps of meditation that I shared with you on Day 5 of Week 4. Also, reflect on the literal and spiritual senses, as you practiced yesterday.

Follow the steps:

1. Put yourself in the presence of God, praising Him with a loving heart.
2. Present yourself humbly before God as you are right now.
3. Read the passage, slowly, absorbing each verse and observing its literal sense.
4. Read the passage a second time, pondering its spiritual sense.
5. Collect your thoughts and stay quietly before God, letting your reflection soak into your soul.
6. Respond to God with a prayer.
7. Think about how to apply your response concretely to your life.
8. Write down the fruit of your reflection and prayer.

Pick one (or more) of the following parables.

> [31b]*The kingdom of heaven is like a mustard seed that someone took and sowed in his field;* [32]*it is the smallest of all the seeds, but when it has grown it is the greatest of shrubs and becomes a tree, so that the birds of the air come and make nests in its branches.* (Mt 13:31b–32)
>
> [33b]*The kingdom of heaven is like yeast that a woman took and mixed in with three measures of flour until all of it was leavened.*
> (Mt 13:33b)

> *[44]The kingdom of heaven is like a treasure hidden in a field, which someone found and hid; then in his joy he goes and sells all that he has and buys that field.* (Mt 13:44)
>
> *[45]The kingdom of heaven is like a merchant in search of fine pearls; [46]on finding one pearl of great value, he went and sold all that he had and bought it.* (Mt 13:45–46)

Pray and meditate on the parable(s), using the steps explained above. When done, write down a summary of your experience.

_____
_____
_____
_____
_____
_____
_____
_____
_____
_____
_____
_____
_____
_____

What is the fruit of your reflection today?

_____
_____
_____
_____
_____

Day 6

This week, I have invited you to come closer to the sacred scriptures and open your heart to the desire to grow in knowledge and friendship with God. I have encouraged you to study the Bible and integrate prayer into your study. Today, you will reflect on the importance of putting the Word of God into practice. Study and prayer with the Bible are important, but more important is to let the Word of God transform your life into the life God wills for you.

> *[46] Why do you call me "Lord, Lord," and do not do what I tell you? [47] I will show you what someone is like who comes to me, hears my words, and acts on them. [48] That one is like a man building a house, who dug deeply and laid the foundation on rock; when a flood arose, the river burst against that house but could not shake it, because it had been well built. [49] But the one who hears and does not act is like a man who built a house on the ground without a foundation. When the river burst against it, immediately it fell, and great was the ruin of that house.* (Lk 6:46–49)

What does it mean to have Jesus as the foundation of your life? Are Jesus's teachings the parameters, the criterion, for your decisions and all you do? Is there anything in your life that is not in accordance with God's will? What can you concretely do to better the "foundation of your house"?

_____

_____

_____

_____

Continue your reflection with the following passage:

> ^{22}Be doers of the word, and not merely hearers who deceive themselves. ^{23}For if any are hearers of the word and not doers, they are like those who look at themselves in a mirror; ^{24}for they look at themselves and, on going away, immediately forget what they were like. ^{25}But those who look into the perfect law, the law of liberty, and persevere, being not hearers who forget but doers who act—they will be blessed in their doing. (Jas 1:22–25)

The perfect law of freedom is love. How does love permeate your actions? In which part of your life is the love of God not the measure of your actions?

_____

_____

_____

_____

_____

The will of God for you is that the love of God be truly perfected in you. This is how we can truly tell we know Jesus.

Read what John says about this in his first letter:

> ^{3}Now by this we may be sure that we know him, if we obey his commandments. ^{4}Whoever says, "I have come to know him," but does not obey his commandments, is a liar, and in such a person the truth does not exist; ^{5}but whoever obeys his word, truly in this person the love of God has reached perfection. By this we may be sure that we are in him: ^{6}whoever says, "I abide in him," ought to walk just as he walked. (1 Jn 2:3–6)

Whatever difficulties you might encounter in living the Word of God, remind yourself that you are not alone in your struggles. The Holy Spirit is within you to help you actualize the life of Jesus in your life.

And every time you receive Jesus in the Eucharist, He makes available to you all the grace you need to conform your life to God's will.

To close your reflection today, read the following passage from the Old Testament that assures that the commandment of the Lord is near and accessible to you.

> *[11] For this command which I am giving you today is not too wondrous or remote for you. [12] It is not in heavens, that you should say, "Who will go up to heavens to get it for us and tell us of it, that we may do it?" [13] Nor is it across the sea, that you should say, "Who will cross the sea to get it for us and tell us of it, that we may do it?" [14] No, it is something very near to you, in your mouth and in your heart, to do it.* (Dt 30:11–14, NAB)

Read verse 14 again and ponder the amazing closeness of the Eucharistic Jesus to your mouth and heart.

Next time you go for Communion, remember verse 14 and pray:

> Dear Jesus, You are so near to me, in my mouth and in my heart, acting in me and giving me the grace I need to love. Thank You, Jesus.

What is the fruit of your reflection today?

_____
_____
_____
_____
_____

Day 7

This week, we journeyed from listening to and knowing the Word of God to acting upon it. Now, to complete the weekly reflection, I invite you to ponder the calling to spread the Word.

The Gospel of Matthew registered the last words of Jesus, right before He ascended into heaven, as a special commission to the apostles.

> [19]*Go therefore and make disciples of all nations, baptizing them in the name of the Father and of the Son and of the Holy Spirit,* [20]*and teaching them to obey everything that I have commanded you. And remember, I am with you always, to the end of the age.* (Mt 28:19–20)

These are meaningful words addressed to the apostles and their successors and to all Christians who participate in the life of the Church and her calling to evangelization. So these words are also for you.

You are called to spread the good news, to announce that, in Jesus, we are saved and are granted the gift of being called children of God.

There are many ways to spread the Word and defend our faith: by deeds, witnessing, intercession for evangelists, and so on. Not all are called to proclaim the Word from a pulpit, but we all need to be ready to seize the opportunities that God presents to us every day.

Let us not miss chances to witness for Jesus due to fear, timidity, embarrassment, or lack of zeal.

The calling to evangelize is especially crucial in times when society and culture grow apart from Christian values.

> [1]*In the presence of God and of Christ Jesus, who is to judge the living and the dead, and in view of his appearing and his kingdom, I*

solemnly urge you: ²proclaim the message; be persistent whether the time is favorable or unfavorable; convince, rebuke, and encourage, with the utmost patience in teaching. ³For the time is coming when people will not put up with sound doctrine, but having itching ears, they will accumulate for themselves teachers to suit their own desires, ⁴and will turn away from listening to the truth and wander away to myths. ⁵As for you, always be sober, endure suffering, do the work of an evangelist, carry out your ministry fully. (2 Tm 4:1–5)

How do you listen to the words of Paul to Timothy? How do you make sense of this advice? Could these words be for you?

Ponder it and write down what God is telling you.

_____
_____
_____
_____
_____

Perhaps you wonder if you are equipped or prepared to proclaim the Word and defend your faith. The truth is, no one is prepared for this task without the assistance of the Holy Spirit.

Before Pentecost, the apostle Peter was a fearful fisherman, but after he received the gift of the Holy Spirit, he was ready to speak the Word with boldness (see Acts 4:31). In Ex 4:10–11 (*NAB*), Moses objected to the commission to lead the people out of Egypt, saying he had speech problems.

"I have never been eloquent, neither in the past nor now that you have spoken to your servant; but I am slow of speech and tongue."

The Lord responded, "Who gives one person speech? . . . Is it not I, the Lord?"

Paul, the greatest missionary of all time, was certain that he had his own limitations and that it was the Holy Spirit who acted on him to speak the Word. Read his testimony and see how it speaks to you.

> *¹When I came to you, brothers and sisters, I did not come proclaiming the mystery of God to you in lofty words or wisdom. ²For I decided to know nothing among you except Jesus Christ, and him crucified. ³And I came to you in weakness and in fear and in much trembling. ⁴My speech and my proclamation were not with plausible words of wisdom, but with a demonstration of the Spirit and of power, ⁵so that your faith might rest not on human wisdom but on the power of God.*
> (1 Cor 2:1–5)

You should never be afraid of speaking out in the name of the Lord. One way or another, we are all called to be missionaries, not with human wisdom and power but with the power of the Holy Spirit.

Keep in mind that God is not interested in human eloquence. Rather, He is looking for humble hearts, people of faith who have given their lives to Christ without reserve and do not look for applause or human recognition.

Are you ready to strip away your fears and human expectations and embrace the mission?

One of the biggest fears people have in evangelizing is that someone might ask them a question they can't answer.

When this occurs, you could simply respond, "That's a good question that I can't answer right now. Let me look into it, and I will get back to you." In so doing, you will also better educate yourself for future evangelizing.

How does your heart react to this reflection? Write down your response in the form of a prayer.

_____
_____
_____
_____

To finish your reflection today, ponder the following verse from the prophet Isaiah. Try to memorize it and keep it close to your heart.

> ⁷How beautiful upon the mountains
> are the feet of the one bringing good news,
> Announcing peace, bearing good news,
> announcing salvation, saying to Zion,
> "Your God is King!" (Is 52:7, NAB)

This week, you have reflected on and prayed with the Word of God. You experienced how to study and pray with the Bible, and you reflected on evangelization. Review your reflections, prayer exercises, and notes from the week and write below what you learned that is new, surprising, or transformative.

_____
_____
_____
_____
_____
_____
_____
_____
_____
_____

Week 6

Service

No one who puts a hand to the plow and looks back is fit for the kingdom of God.
(Lk 9:62b)

Day 1

This week, we will reflect on our calling to serve in the Kingdom of God.

Before exploring how we can personally serve the Lord, let us spend some time contemplating the most perfect model of servant.

About seven hundred years before Christ was born, Isaiah prophesied that the Lord would send a servant who would suffer and triumph for the sins and justification of many.

This prophecy is fulfilled in Jesus, the suffering servant of the Lord.

To learn about this prophecy, you can read the whole passage from Isaiah 52:13–53:12 in your Bible. However, for our reflection today, I invite you to ponder a few select verses.

> *^{13}See, my servant shall prosper,*
> *he shall be raised high and greatly exalted.*
> *^{14}Even as many were amazed at him—*
> *so marred were his features,*
> *beyond that of mortals*
> *his appearances, beyond that of human beings—*
> *^{15}So shall he startle many nations,*
> *kings shall stand speechless;*
> *For those who have not been told shall see,*
> *those who have not heard shall ponder it.* (Is 52:13–15, *NAB*)

> *^{3}He was spurned and avoided by men,*
> *a man of suffering, knowing pain,*
> *Like one from whom you turn your face,*
> *spurned, and we held him in no esteem. . . .*

> *⁷Though harshly treated, he submitted*
> *and did not open his mouth;*
> *Like a lamb led to slaughter*
> *or a sheep silent before shearers,*
> *he did not open his mouth. . . .*
> *¹⁰But it was the LORD's will to crush him with pain.*
> *By making his life as a reparation offering,*
> *he shall see his offering, shall lengthen his days,*
> *and the LORD's will shall be accomplished through him. . . .*
> *¹¹ᵇMy servant, the just one, shall justify the many,*
> *their iniquity he shall bear.*
> *¹²Therefore I will give him his portion among the many,*
> *and he shall divide the spoils with the mighty,*
> *Because he surrendered himself to death,*
> *was counted among the transgressors,*
> *Bore the sins of many,*
> *and interceded for the transgressors.*
> (Is 53:3, 7, 10, 11b–12, *NAB*)

Jesus fulfilled this prophecy by making Himself a servant and surrendering His life for us. Being God with the Father, He came to us as a humble servant. In the Kingdom of God, to serve means to give one's life for others out of love.

Having Jesus as our model of servant, let us reflect on what Paul wrote to the Philippians.

> *⁵Have among yourselves the same attitude that is also yours in Christ Jesus,*
> *⁶Who, though he was in the form of God,*
> *did not regard equality with God something to be grasped.*
> *⁷Rather, he emptied himself*
> *taking the form of a slave,*
> *coming in human likeness;*
> *and found human in appearance,*
> *⁸he humbled himself,*
> *becoming obedient to death, even death on a cross.*
> *⁹Because of this, God greatly exalted him*

and bestowed on him the name
that is above every name,
¹⁰that at the name of Jesus
every knee should bend,
of those in heaven and on earth and under the earth,
¹¹and every tongue confess that
Jesus Christ is Lord,
to the glory of God the Father. (Phil 2:5–11, *NAB*)

Jesus is Lord, but a Lord who chose to be a servant. What can you tell Jesus when you contemplate His choice? Write down your reflection in the form of a prayer.

_____
_____
_____
_____

Are you ready to be a servant following in Jesus's footsteps? Are you ready to give your life for others? How can you apply this kind of love to your life?

_____
_____
_____
_____

Can you do it by yourself? Do you feel afraid? Inadequate? Confused? Do you think you need the help of the Holy Spirit to be a humble servant in the Kingdom of God? What, then, is your petition to God?

_____
_____
_____

Week 6

What is the fruit of your reflection today?

_____
_____
_____
_____
_____

Day 2

Today, I invite you to reflect on the calling and response of a beautiful and humble human being who, by the grace of God, was the most perfect servant of the Lord.

Let us look at the example of the Virgin Mary and pray for her maternal assistance to help us respond to our calling to serve.

Let us ponder Mary's response to the angel Gabriel right after the announcement of the coming birth of Jesus:

> *38aThen Mary said, "Here am I, the servant of the Lord; let it be with me according to your word." (Lk 1:38a)*

Mary is the servant of the Lord. From her, we can learn about humility and obedience to the will of God. She was a faithful servant throughout her whole life.

On the day she received the visit from the angel Gabriel, she did not stay self-absorbed with the announcement. Completely detached from self, as soon as she knew her cousin Elizabeth had conceived in her old age, Mary traveled to help her out and stayed with Elizabeth for three months.

> *39In those days Mary set out and went with haste to a Judean town in the hill country, 40where she entered the house of Zechariah and greeted Elizabeth.*
>
> *56And Mary remained with her about three months and then returned to her home. (Lk 1:39–40, 56)*

Let us pray with the canticle Mary proclaimed when she greeted Elizabeth. Read slowly, verse by verse, and stay with the verse that speaks to you. Let the verse soak into your soul for a while. Then talk to Mary about it.

> ^{46} *And Mary said:*
> *"My soul proclaims the greatness of the Lord;*
> ^{47} *my spirit rejoices in God my savior.*
> ^{48} *For he has looked upon his handmaid's lowliness;*
> *behold, from now on will all ages call me blessed.*
> ^{49} *The Mighty One has done great things for me,*
> *and holy is his name.*
> ^{50} *His mercy is from age to age*
> *to those who fear him.*
> ^{51} *He has shown might with his arm,*
> *dispersed the arrogant of mind and heart.*
> ^{52} *He has thrown down the rulers from their thrones*
> *but lifted up the lowly.*
> ^{53} *The hungry he has filled with good things;*
> *the rich he has sent away empty.*
> ^{54} *He has helped Israel his servant,*
> *remembering his mercy,*
> ^{55} *according to his promise to our fathers,*
> *to Abraham and to his descendants forever."* (Lk 1:46–55, *NAB*)

Write down your prayer to our heavenly Mother. If you do not have the habit of talking to Mary often, then tell her about that.

_____
_____
_____
_____
_____

Continue your prayer:

> Dear heavenly Mother, you have the purest heart. You completely abandoned yourself in the hands of the Father and

made yourself completely available to serve according to God's will. You know all about surrendering one's life in the service of God. Please, teach me to open up to serve the Lord. I want to be a faithful servant like you. Sweet Mary, help me and guide me with your maternal love. Pray for me and ask Jesus, your beloved son, to pour the Holy Spirit into my heart so I might serve Him with joy, love, kindness, and generosity. Thank you, my dearest Mary. Hail Mary, full of grace, the Lord is with you. Blessed are you among women, and blessed is the fruit of your womb, Jesus. Holy Mary, Mother of God, pray for us sinners, now and at the hour of our death. Amen.

What is the fruit of your reflection today?

_____
_____
_____
_____
_____

Day 3

Today, I invite you to meditate with a passage from the Gospel of John, the washing of the feet.

You will read this passage three times. As you first read the passage, observe the details of the event. Familiarize yourself with the scene; imagine the room, the disciples, and Jesus with a towel and a basin full of water. Listen to the dialogues.

> ^{1}It was just before the Passover Festival. Jesus knew that the hour had come for him to leave this world and go to the Father. Having loved his own who were in the world, he loved them to the end. ^{2}The evening meal was in progress, and the devil had already prompted Judas, the son of Simon Iscariot, to betray Jesus. ^{3}Jesus knew that the Father had put all things under his power, and that he had come from God and was returning to God; ^{4}so he got up from the meal, took off his outer clothing, and wrapped a towel around his waist. ^{5}After that, he poured water into a basin and began to wash his disciples' feet, drying them with the towel that was wrapped around him. ^{6}He came to Simon Peter, who said to him, "Lord, are you going to wash my feet?" ^{7}Jesus replied, "You do not realize now what I am doing, but later you will understand." ^{8}"No," said Peter, "you shall never wash my feet." Jesus answered, "Unless I wash you, you have no part with me." ^{9}"Then, Lord," Simon Peter replied, "not just my feet but my hands and my head as well!" ^{10}Jesus answered, "Those who have had a bath need only to wash their feet; their whole body is clean. And you are clean, though not every one of you." ^{11}For he knew who was going to betray him, and that was why he said not every one was clean. ^{12}When he had finished washing their feet, he put on his clothes and returned to his place. "Do you understand what I have done for you?" he asked them. ^{13}"You call me 'Teacher' and 'Lord,' and rightly so, for that is what I

am. ¹⁴Now that I, your Lord and Teacher, have washed your feet, you also should wash one another's feet. ¹⁵I have set you an example that you should do as I have done for you. ¹⁶Very truly I tell you, no servant is greater than his master, nor is a messenger greater than the one who sent him. ¹⁷Now that you know these things, you will be blessed if you do them. (Jn 13:1–17, *NIV*)

Now, read the passage a second time. This time, imagine yourself among the disciples, taking the place of Peter. Imagine your thoughts and feelings as Jesus approaches you and speaks to you, face to face. Write down what stands out to you in your interaction with Jesus.

_____
_____
_____
_____

Now, read the passage a third time. As you read, take the place of Jesus. Imagine that you are getting prepared to wash the disciples' feet. Wash their feet. Look at their faces. Who do you see in their faces? What are your feelings as you wash their feet?

_____
_____
_____
_____

Review your experience as you meditate on the washing of the feet and write down your response to God.

_____
_____
_____
_____

What is the fruit of your reflection today?

_____
_____
_____
_____
_____

Day 4

We have reflected on Jesus as the servant of the Lord. We have understood that the context of His service is His death and resurrection. In other words, the glorification of Jesus as Lord comes through the cross.

Jesus, our model of servant, is teaching us that service is about giving one's life for others.

> *^{24}Then Jesus told his disciples, "If any want to become my followers, let them deny themselves and take up their cross and follow me. ^{25}For those who want to save their life will lose it, and those who lose their life for my sake will find it."* (Mt 16:24–25)

There is no glory without the cross; there is no cross without self-sacrificing. It is within this context that service in the Kingdom of God makes sense.

How easily we forget what service really is! It is important to open up to service and be ready to serve, but it is fundamental to serve with the right inner disposition.

Service has nothing to do with positions where one can be in the spotlight and receive applause and recognition. Service requires humility. In the Kingdom of God, there is no place for the leaven of vainglory and pride.

Today, I invite you to ponder the inner disposition of your heart when serving the Lord.

> *^{20}Then the mother of the sons of Zebedee came to him with her sons, and kneeling before him, she asked a favor of him. ^{21}And he said to her, "What do you want?" She said to him, "Declare that these two*

sons of mine will sit, one at your right hand and one at your left, in your kingdom." ²²But Jesus answered, "You do not know what you are asking. Are you able to drink the cup that I am about to drink?" They said to him, "We are able." ²³He said to them, "You will indeed drink my cup, but to sit at my right hand and at my left, this is not mine to grant, but it is for those for whom it has been prepared by my Father." ²⁴When the ten heard it, they were angry with the two brothers. ²⁵But Jesus called them to him and said, "You know that the rulers of the Gentiles lord it over them, and their great ones are tyrants over them. ²⁶It will not be so among you; but whoever wishes to be great among you must be your servant, ²⁷and whoever wishes to be first among you must be your slave; ²⁸just as the Son of Man came not to be served but to serve, and to give his life a ransom for many."
(Mt 20:20–28)

How do you react to this passage? Does it have anything to do with you? Do you feel more like the sons of Zebedee or like the other ten who became indignant? How so?

_____
_____
_____
_____

How can you apply this passage to your life? How do you respond to Jesus, who calls you to be a servant?

_____
_____
_____
_____

One final thought for you to consider: we are not called to serve in exchange for earthly rewards.

We should not expect anything from other people nor from God. God will continue to pour His grace upon us as He wills, but not because we deserve them in exchange for our good services. His grace is a free gift; it is not a reward for our service.

Jesus gave His life freely, out of love. In the same way, our motivation to serve should be freely given love. We are not entitled employees; we are humble servants of the most loving Lord.

All that really matters—salvation and eternal life—is already given to us.

> *[1b]The LORD is my shepherd;*
> *there is nothing I lack.* (Ps 23:1b, NAB)

Read the following text and ponder it.

> *[7]Who among you would say to your slave who has just come in from plowing or tending sheep in the field, "Come here at once and take your place at the table"? [8]Would you not rather say to him, "Prepare supper for me, put on your apron and serve me while I eat and drink; later you may eat and drink"? [9]Do you thank the slave for doing what was commanded? [10]So you also, when you have done all that you were ordered to do, say, "We are worthless slaves; we have done only what we ought to have done!"* (Lk 17:7–10)

What is God telling you through this passage? What is your response?

_____
_____
_____
_____
_____

Week 6

What is the fruit of your reflection today?

_____
_____
_____
_____
_____

Day 5

Jesus gave Himself freely. He embraced the cross, totally moved by His love for us. In the same way, service in the Kingdom of God is more meaningful when it comes from the heart. Freely responding to the calling reflects the desire of a heart that has been deeply touched by the love of God.

To delve into this reflection, consider the following passage, in which Jesus performs a healing.

> *[14]When Jesus entered Peter's house, he saw his mother-in-law lying in bed with a fever; [15]he touched her hand, and the fever left her, and she got up and began to serve him.* (Mt 8:14–15)

What a great experience it must have been to have such a personal and intimate encounter with Jesus! And what a great privilege, for Peter's mother-in-law to serve Jesus personally! Service springs from the healing touch of Jesus. I can only imagine the joy and gratitude she experienced.

How would you feel, putting yourself in the place of Peter's mother-in-law?

_____

_____

_____

_____

Let us stay with those verses and pray.

> Dear Jesus, touch me. Touch my hand, touch my heart, touch my mind. Touch wherever in me that needs to be

healed by Your love so that I can get up, get out of my comfort zone, get out of my selfishness, and be ready to serve. Grant me the gift of service. Let me experience the joy of serving out of love and expecting nothing in return. Your love is all I need, my precious Jesus. I want nothing else, as long I have You in my life. Thank You for calling me to serve. Amen.

We may not have the privilege of serving Jesus personally, as Peter's mother-in-law did, but we certainly have daily opportunities to serve the hidden Jesus within others.

There is great joy in serving Jesus through our brothers and sisters in need. Ponder this as you read the parable Jesus told about the final judgment.

> *^{34}Then the king will say to those at his right hand, "Come, you that are blessed by my Father, inherit the kingdom prepared for you from the foundation of the world; ^{35}for I was hungry and you gave me food, I was thirsty and you gave me something to drink, I was a stranger and you welcomed me, ^{36}I was naked and you gave me clothing, I was sick and you took care of me, I was in prison and you visited me." ^{37}Then the righteous will answer him, "Lord, when was it that we saw you hungry and gave you food, or thirsty and gave you something to drink? ^{38}And when was it that we saw you a stranger and welcomed you, or naked and gave you clothing? ^{39}And when was it that we saw you sick or in prison and visited you?" ^{40}And the king will answer them, "Truly I tell you, just as you did it to one of the least of these who are members of my family, you did it to me."* (Mt 25:34–40)

How do you react to this passage? What is your response to God?

_____
_____
_____
_____

Read the following verses to conclude today's reflection. Try to keep this passage close to your heart for the rest of the day:

> *[16] We know love by this, that he laid down his life for us—and we ought to lay down our lives for one another. [17] How does God's love abide in anyone who has the world's goods and sees a brother or sister in need and yet refuses help?*
>
> *[18] Little children, let us love, not in word or speech, but in truth and action. (1 Jn 3:16–18)*

What is the fruit of your reflection today?

_____
_____
_____
_____
_____

Day 6

As we move forward in our reflections on the attitudes we should have when serving the Lord, it becomes clear that it is not a task we can do on our own and with our own resources. We are incapable of being the servants God wants us to be unless the Holy Spirit comes to our rescue and puts the love of God in our hearts. Without the assistance of the Holy Spirit, we are useless for service in the Kingdom of God.

Let us pray, humbly and sincerely.

> Come, Holy Spirit. Blow Your grace upon me. Kindle my soul with Your fire and cleanse me so I can serve the Lord with a pure heart. Give me the grace to find joy in serving with freedom and detachment. Touch my mind so I can understand the true meaning of service. Touch my heart so I can love Jesus with all my heart and soul and let me see His face in the faces of my brothers and sisters in need. Let the love of God flow through me so I can serve the Lord with the same love that moved Jesus to serve. Amen.

The Holy Spirit prepares us to become faithful servants. He distributes His gifts among us so we can serve one another and participate in the building of the Church, which is the Kingdom of God on Earth.

The following passages were addressed to the Christians of the early Church. They were still learning how to serve and build community with the assistance of the Holy Spirit.

Consider this: We are not disconnected pieces of a broken machine, each working on its own without a common purpose. Rather, we are parts of one body, a unity, looking at the same goal in Jesus Christ and moved by the grace of God to bring light into this world.

Ponder this as you read the following passages.

> *⁴Now there are varieties of gifts, but the same Spirit; ⁵and there are varieties of services, but the same Lord; ⁶and there are varieties of activities, but it is the same God who activates all of them in everyone. ⁷To each is given the manifestation of the Spirit for the common good.* (1 Cor 12:4–7)

> *¹⁰Like good stewards of the manifold grace of God, serve one another with whatever gift each of you has received. ¹¹Whoever speaks must do so as one speaking the very words of God; whoever serves must do so with the strength that God supplies, so that God may be glorified in all things through Jesus Christ. To him belong the glory and the power forever and ever. Amen.* (1 Pt 4:10–11)

> *³For by the grace given to me I say to everyone among you not to think of yourself more highly than you ought to think, but to think with sober judgment, each according to the measure of faith that God has assigned. ⁴For as in one body we have many members, and not all the members have the same function, ⁵so we, who are many, are one body in Christ, and individually we are members one of another. ⁶We have gifts that differ according to the grace given to us: prophecy, in proportion to faith; ⁷ministry, in ministering; the teacher, in teaching; ⁸the exhorter, in exhortation; the giver, in generosity; the leader, in diligence; the compassionate, in cheerfulness.* (Rom 12:3–8)

Which verse calls your attention the most? What is God telling you with this verse?

_____
_____
_____
_____

What is your response to God?

_____
_____
_____
_____
_____

How can you concretely apply your reflection to your life?

_____
_____
_____
_____
_____

Once the Holy Spirit has set our hearts on fire with the desire to serve, we might wonder what our specific calling is. Are we called to serve by deeds of mercy and almsgiving? By a committed life of prayer and intercession? By proclaiming the gospel to those who hunger and thirst for the Word of God? By engaging in an active parish ministry? Or by witnessing for Christ in our family and workplace?

What is your specific calling? What is the gift the Holy Spirit has given you to serve?

_____
_____
_____
_____
_____

What is the fruit of your reflection today?

_____
_____
_____
_____
_____

Day 7

Based on our reflections this week, we can come to the conclusion that service is not about something one does but rather about being like Jesus, the model of servant to the Lord.

God is less interested in the results or the product of our service than in the transformation of our hearts in becoming faithful and true servants.

The words of Samuel addressed to Saul in the Old Testament can bring light to our reflection today.

> [22]*But Samuel said:*
> *"Does the LORD delight in burnt offerings and sacrifices*
> *as much as in obedience to the LORD's command?*
> *Obedience is better than sacrifice,*
> *to listen, better than the fat of rams."* (1 Sm 15:22, NAB)

Does this verse speak to you? How? What is your response?

_____
_____
_____
_____
_____

Now, read the following passage to conclude your reflection. Read it as if Paul were a very close and caring friend of yours and had written this letter especially for you.

^{12}Therefore, my beloved, just as you have always obeyed me, not only in my presence, but much more now in my absence, work out your own salvation with fear and trembling; ^{13}for it is God who is at work in you, enabling you both to will and to work for his good pleasure.

^{14}Do all things without murmuring and arguing, ^{15}so that you may be blameless and innocent, children of God without blemish in the midst of a crooked and perverse generation, in which you shine like stars in the world. ^{16}It is by your holding fast to the word of life that I can boast on the day of Christ that I did not run in vain or labor in vain. ^{17}But even if I am being poured out as a libation over the sacrifice and the offering of your faith, I am glad and rejoice with all of you— ^{18}and in the same way you also must be glad and rejoice with me.
(Phil 2:12–18)

How would you write a letter to your friend Paul in reply? Do you have comments? Questions? Needs that you would like to share with him?

_____
_____
_____
_____
_____
_____
_____
_____
_____
_____

During this week, you have considered what service really is. You have opened up to the Holy Spirit, to let it transform your heart into the heart of a true servant. At this point, ready as you are, Jesus wants to bring you to the next level.

I invite you to cherish with great joy the following verses from the Gospel of John.

> *^{14}You are my friends if you do what I command you. ^{15}I do not call you servants any longer, because the servant does not know what the master is doing; but I have called you friends, because I have made known to you everything that I have heard from my Father.*
> (Jn 15:14–15)

No longer servants, but friends! How awesome is our God!

This week, you have reflected on and prayed about the meaning of service in the Kingdom of God. You reflected on our model of servant and the calling to serve. Review your reflections, prayer exercises, and notes from the week and write below what you learned that is new, surprising, or transformative.

_____
_____
_____
_____
_____
_____
_____
_____
_____
_____

Week 7

Sacraments

I am with you always, to the end of the age.
(Mt 28:20b)

Day 1

The word *sacrament* means "sign." Each of the seven sacraments (Baptism, Confirmation, Eucharist, Penance and Reconciliation, Anointing of the Sick, Holy Orders, and Matrimony) is a sign assuring us that Jesus is alive and acting in His Church.

Jesus Himself operates the proper grace of each sacrament. When we fully live the sacraments, we share in the divine life of Jesus as true children of God.

The sacraments, through the Holy Spirit, provide us with the grace and gifts we need for our personal sanctification, the strengthening of our faith and disposition to serve and build the Church.

Baptism, Confirmation, and Eucharist are the sacraments of Christian initiation.

Baptism is the gateway to the Christian life. It is the rebirth of the old person, marked by the original sin, into a new person, regenerated by Christ.

> ^{1}*Now there was a Pharisee named Nicodemus, a leader of the Jews.* ^{2}*He came to Jesus by night and said to him, "Rabbi, we know that you are a teacher who has come from God; for no one can do these signs that you do apart from the presence of God."* ^{3}*Jesus answered him, "Very truly, I tell you, no one can see the kingdom of God without being born from above."* ^{4}*Nicodemus said to him, "How can anyone be born after having grown old? Can one enter a second time into the mother's womb and be born?"* ^{5}*Jesus answered, "Very truly, I tell you, no one can enter the kingdom of God without being born of water and Spirit."* (Jn 3:1–5)

Every human being is born tainted with the original sin that leads to eternal death. The waters of Baptism cleanse us of the original sin and free us from death. Christ's death and resurrection granted us the rebirth of a new life. Through the sacrament of Baptism, we receive this grace.

In the Old Testament, we see prefigurements of the sacrament of Baptism, in which water, death, and redemption points to Christ's death and resurrection.

The people in Noah's ark were saved, while the waters of the great flood cleansed the surface of a world full of iniquity (see Gn 6–7). The crossing of the Red Sea was the death of slavery in Egypt and represents liberation from sin (see Ex 14), while the crossing of the Jordan River was the entrance into the Promised Land, which represents the eternal life, our final destination (see Jos 3).

In Christ, we are immersed in the waters of Baptism, to rise as free children of God.

Ponder this with the following passage.

> *²How can we who died to sin go on living in it? ³Do you not know that all of us who have been baptized into Christ Jesus were baptized into his death? ⁴Therefore we have been buried with him by baptism into death, so that, just as Christ was raised from the dead by the glory of the Father, so we too might walk in newness of life.* (Rom 6:2–4)

Consider that the grace received through Baptism is an absolutely free gift, given when one is totally bound by original sin.

It is only through this grace that one is regenerated. It regenerates newborn children, who have not committed personal sins (which are different from the original sin), and adults, who have experienced mortal or venial sins.

> *³For we ourselves were once foolish, disobedient, deluded, slaves to various desires and pleasures, living in malice and envy, hateful ourselves and hating one another.*

> ⁴*But when the kindness and generous love*
> *of God our savior appeared,*
> ⁵*not because of any righteous deeds we had done*
> *but because of his mercy,*
> *he saved us through the bath of rebirth*
> *and renewal by the holy Spirit,*
> ⁶*whom he richly poured out on us*
> *through Jesus Christ our savior,*
> ⁷*so that we might be justified by his grace*
> *and become heirs in hope of eternal life.* (Ti 3:3–7, NAB)

Consider how merciful God is in giving us such grace! Consider also that even though the sacrament of Baptism is received only once, we can always ask the Holy Spirit to renew the baptismal grace.

What is your response to this?

_____
_____
_____

Be assured that the Holy Spirit operates in you a constant renewal, transforming you in Christ in the measure of your faith, hope, and love.

Read the following verse and save it in your heart to ponder for the rest of your day.

> ²⁷*For all of you who were baptized into Christ have clothed yourselves with Christ.* (Gal 3:27, NAB)

What is the fruit of your reflection today?

_____
_____
_____
_____

Day 2

Confirmation is the sacrament that strengthens and completes the baptismal grace, leading the baptized to the fullness of the Holy Spirit.

Start your reflection today by reading and pondering the following passage.

> [14]Now when the apostles at Jerusalem heard that Samaria had accepted the word of God, they sent Peter and John to them. [15]The two went down and prayed for them that they might receive the Holy Spirit [16](for as yet the Spirit had not come upon any of them; they had only been baptized in the name of the Lord Jesus). [17]Then Peter and John laid their hands on them, and they received the Holy Spirit.
> (Acts 8:14–17)

What stands out to you in this passage? Inspired by this reading, what would be your petitions to God?

_____

_____

_____

_____

By the sacrament of Confirmation, the Holy Spirit seals the Christian. When we receive the laying on of hands and are anointed with oil, we are consecrated—that is, marked by the Holy Spirit with the sign of belonging to God.

Ponder the following verses.

> *¹³In him you also, when you had heard the word of truth, the gospel of your salvation, and had believed in him, were marked with the seal of the promised Holy Spirit; ¹⁴this is the pledge of our inheritance toward redemption as God's own people, to the praise of his glory.*
> (Eph 1:13–14)

> *²²He has also put his seal upon us and given the Spirit in our hearts as a first installment.* (2 Cor 1:22, NAB)

Through Confirmation, the Holy Spirit is given to us to help us grow spiritually. The following passage from Isaiah refers to Jesus, who was the promised descendant of King David. But it also refers to you, for Jesus has poured His Spirit into you through Baptism and wants to give you the fullness of the Holy Spirit through Confirmation.

> *¹But a shoot shall sprout from the stump of Jesse,
> and from the roots a bud shall blossom.
> ²The spirit of the LORD shall rest upon him:
> a spirit of wisdom and of understanding,
> A spirit of counsel and of strength,
> a spirit of knowledge and of fear of the LORD.*
> (Is 11:1–2, NAB)

Do you accept being sealed by the Holy Spirit and belonging to God above all else? Which gifts of the Holy Spirit (based on the passage above) do you need in order to improve your spiritual growth?

_____
_____
_____
_____
_____

Along with your spiritual growth, another effect of the sacrament of Confirmation is to give you strength and send you on a mission as a true soldier of Christ and His Church.

In the next passage, Isaiah refers to Jesus, but also to those who are sealed to spread the gospel and witness for Christ.

Read the following passage twice. First, open your heart to receive grace from Christ through the Holy Spirit. Then read it again, allowing the Holy Spirit to use you as an instrument of God to bring good news to others.

> *¹The spirit of the Lord GOD is upon me,*
> *because the LORD has anointed me;*
> *He has sent me to bring good news to the afflicted,*
> *to bind up the brokenhearted,*
> *To proclaim liberty to the captives,*
> *release the prisoners,*
> *²To announce a year of favor from the LORD*
> *and a day of vindication by our God;*
> *To comfort all who mourn;*
> *³to place on those who mourn in Zion*
> *a diadem instead of ashes,*
> *To give them oil of gladness instead of mourning,*
> *a glorious mantle instead of a faint spirit.*
>
> *They will be called oaks of justice,*
> *the planting of the LORD to show his glory.*
> (Is 61:1–3, *NAB*)

What is God telling you through this passage? What is your response to God?

_____

_____

_____

_____

_____

Confirmation, like Baptism, is received only once. However, you can always ask the Holy Spirit for a renewal of its grace.

If you, or someone you love, have not received the sacrament of Confirmation yet, I encourage you to consider receiving it. What would be your next steps to make sure you do not miss out on this special grace?

_____

_____

_____

_____

_____

What is the fruit of your reflection today?

_____

_____

_____

_____

_____

Day 3

Eucharist is the sacrament that completes the Christian initiation. It is the Sacrament of all sacraments, the Most Blessed Sacrament, because it is Christ Himself, the center of our faith and the life of the Church.

In the Eucharist, Jesus gives Himself to us as food to be eaten. When we eat something, it becomes incorporated in our bodies, totally united with our bodies. This is how united with us Jesus wants to be.

I invite you to ponder this most amazing mystery of our faith as you read the following passage from the Gospel of John. Consider the seriousness of Jesus's words when He reveals Himself as the bread of life.

> [31] *"Our ancestors ate the manna in the wilderness; as it is written: 'He gave them bread from heaven to eat.'"* [32] *Jesus said to them, "Very truly I tell you, it is not Moses who has given you the bread from heaven, but it is my Father who gives you the true bread from heaven.* [33] *For the bread of God is the bread that comes down from heaven and gives life to the world."* [34] *"Sir," they said, "always give us this bread."* [35] *Then Jesus declared, "I am the bread of life. Whoever comes to me will never go hungry, and whoever believes in me will never be thirsty."*
>
> [52] *Then the Jews began to argue sharply among themselves, "How can this man give us his flesh to eat?"* [53] *Jesus said to them, "Very truly I tell you, unless you eat the flesh of the Son of Man and drink his blood, you have no life in you.* [54] *Whoever eats my flesh and drinks my blood has eternal life, and I will raise them up at the last day.* [55] *For my flesh is real food and my blood is real drink.* [56] *Whoever eats my flesh and drinks my blood remains in me, and I in them."*
>
> (Jn 6:31–35, 52–56, *NIV*)

What stands out to you as most important in this passage? Did you notice that when the Jews quarreled, Jesus did not dismiss His words as metaphors but, on the contrary, reaffirmed them in their literal meaning? Jesus was more concerned about the truth of His body and blood than about being popular with the Jews.

Can you accept the importance of His words? What is your reaction? How do you respond to God?

_____

_____

_____

_____

The Old Testament points to the Eucharist in many ways, such as the manna in the desert (see Ex 16:4) and the unleavened bread of the Passover (see Ex 12:8). Jesus also anticipates the Eucharist in the miracle of the multiplication of the loaves when He feeds the hungry crowd (see Mt 14:15–21).

However, the most astonishing foreshadowing of the Eucharist is the sacrifice of the Passover lamb that the Jews celebrated every year (see Ex 12).

During the Last Supper, for the occasion of Passover, Jesus initiated His ultimate sacrifice for us, which culminated on the cross. Jesus is the Lamb sacrificed for our sins, who shed His blood so that we could be saved from death.

Just like the lamb of the Old Covenant, which had to be eaten in this sacred ritual, Jesus, the new sacrificial Lamb, gave His flesh to be eaten. In this way, He inaugurated the liturgical meal of the New Covenant.

Ponder this as you read the next passage.

> *²⁶While they were eating, Jesus took a loaf of bread, and after blessing it he broke it, gave it to the disciples, and said, "Take, eat; this is my body." ²⁷Then he took a cup, and after giving thanks he gave it to*

> them, saying, "Drink from it, all of you; ²⁸for this is my blood of the covenant, which is poured out for many for the forgiveness of sins."
> (Mt 26:26–28)

How do you feel about partaking of the meal of the New Covenant, which takes place at every Mass that is celebrated? Do you feel nourished by this divine meal? Have you ever thought about the great honor it is to receive Jesus Himself within you?

Ponder these questions and write your prayer as a response to God.

_____

_____

_____

_____

On the road to Emmaus, the disciples were able to recognize Jesus when He explained to them the scriptures and broke bread with them.

> ²⁷*Then beginning with Moses and all the prophets, he interpreted to them the things about himself in all the scriptures.*
>
> ³⁰*When he was at the table with them, he took bread, blessed and broke it, and gave it to them.* ³¹*Then their eyes were opened, and they recognized him; and he vanished from their sight.* ³²*They said to each other, "Were not our hearts burning within us while he was talking to us on the road, while he was opening the scriptures to us?"*
> (Lk 24:27, 30–32)

Since the apostles in the early Christian community, the Catholic Church has been faithful to Jesus, who said, "Do this in remembrance of me" (1 Cor 11:24). Up to this day and all over the world, the liturgy of the Mass is celebrated with the proclamation of the Word of God and the Eucharist.

> *⁴²They devoted themselves to the teaching of the apostles and to the communal life, to the breaking of the bread and to the prayers.* (Acts 2:42, NAB)

Through the Eucharist, Jesus wants to communicate His divine life to us and grant us the grace of unity. As the Trinity is One, Christ wants us to be One with Him and One as a Church, united to Him in perfect communion.

> *¹⁷Because there is one bread, we who are many are one body, for we all partake of the one bread.* (1 Cor 10:17)

As a final reflection, consider these two great miracles: By the power of the Holy Spirit, the Son was made flesh in the womb of Mary. What a great miracle! Then in the Eucharist, Jesus gives His flesh to us in the appearance of bread so we can have His life in us. The Eucharist is the perfected miracle of Incarnation.

Considering such great miracles, can you imagine what God has prepared for us in heaven? Until then, we continue celebrating the Eucharist as we await the final Passover in heaven.

Let us finish today's reflection with the anticipation of the Eucharist in heaven, when we, the Church, will be totally united with Christ and immersed in the life of the Trinity.

> *⁹Then the angel said to me, "Write this: Blessed are those who have been called to the wedding feast of the Lamb." And he said to me, "These words are true; they come from God."* (Rev 19:9, NAB)

What is the fruit of your reflection today?

_____

_____

_____

_____

_____

Day 4

There are two sacraments of healing: the sacrament of Penance and Reconciliation, and the sacrament of the Anointing of the Sick. Today, let us consider the sacrament of Penance and Reconciliation, also known as the sacrament of Confession.

The sacraments of Christian initiation (Baptism, Confirmation, and Eucharist) give us the grace of a new life in Christ. However, we continue to struggle with our inclination to sin, and we need constant conversion to a Christian life.

Sometimes, like the prodigal son, we stray away and end up in need of a new conversion. Coming to our senses, we start our journey back home to find the forgiving arms of the Father.

The sacrament of Reconciliation is the healing we need to start over.

> *^{17}But when he came to himself he said, "How many of my father's hired hands have bread enough and to spare, but here I am dying of hunger! ^{18}I will get up and go to my father, and I will say to him, 'Father, I have sinned against heaven and before you; ^{19}I am no longer worthy to be called your son; treat me like one of your hired hands.'" ^{20}So he set off and went to his father. But while he was still far off, his father saw him and was filled with compassion; he ran and put his arms around him and kissed him. ^{21}Then the son said to him, "Father, I have sinned against heaven and before you; I am no longer worthy to be called your son." ^{22}But the father said to his slaves, "Quickly, bring out a robe—the best one—and put it on him; put a ring on his finger and sandals on his feet. ^{23}And get the fatted calf and kill it, and let us eat and celebrate; ^{24}for this son of mine was dead and is alive again; he was lost and is found!" And they began to celebrate.*
> (Lk 15:17–24)

Can you identify with the prodigal son?

Think about a time when you realized the error of your ways and experienced the compassion and forgiveness of the Father. How did it feel?

Where are you right now, in distant lands or in the arms of the Father? Write down your reflection.

_____

_____

_____

_____

_____

We will always be sinners in need of forgiveness, and our merciful God will always be waiting for us with compassion. However, it is important to repent with sincere sorrow.

Peter is an example of true contrition.

> *[61]The Lord turned and looked at Peter. Then Peter remembered the word of the Lord, how he had said to him, "Before the cock crows today, you will deny me three times." [62]And he went out and wept bitterly.* (Lk 22:61–62)

Peter was deeply sorry because he had offended Jesus. When we sin, we offend Jesus, who died on the cross for our sins.

Inspired by the following passage from Zechariah, I invite you to take a moment to reflect on your sins. Then look at Jesus on the cross and ask the Holy Spirit to give you the grace of perfect contrition.

> *[10]I will pour out on the house of David and on the inhabitants of Jerusalem a spirit of mercy and supplication, so that when they look on him whom they have thrust through, they will mourn for him as one*

mourns for an only child, and they will grieve for him as one grieves over a firstborn. (Zec 12:10, *NAB*)

Once you are sincerely sorry for your sins and have the firm resolution to make amends, the next step toward reconciliation is the confession.

^{13}Those who conceal their sins do not prosper, but those who confess and forsake them obtain mercy. (Prv 28:13, *NAB*)

^{9}If we confess our sins, he who is faithful and just will forgive us our sins and cleanse us from all unrighteousness. (1 Jn 1:9)

To receive the grace of the sacrament, it is necessary to confess to a priest, who, in the name and authority of Jesus, will grant you forgiveness.

Consider the following passages, which show that Jesus had the clear intention to give the apostles and their successors a special authority to forgive sins.

^{21}[Jesus] said to them again, "Peace be with you. As the Father has sent me, so I send you." ^{22}And when he had said this, he breathed on them and said to them, "Receive the holy Spirit. ^{23}Whose sins you forgive are forgiven them, and whose sins you retain are retained." (Jn 20:21–23, *NAB*)

^{19}I will give you the keys of the kingdom of heaven, and whatever you bind on earth will be bound in heaven, and whatever you loose on earth will be loosed in heaven. (Mt 16:19)

It is not the priest who forgives you. Only God can forgive sins. It is God, through the priest, who forgives you, so it does not matter if the priest is a sinner like you. You will receive the grace of the sacrament because Jesus is true and faithful to His promises.

Even though we have been forgiven of our sins, we still have to repair the broken relationship between God and us. For that, the priest will prescribe us penance when we receive the sacrament of Reconciliation.

Sometimes, repentance and confession of sins requires reparation to someone who was harmed by our sins.

> *⁸Zacchaeus stood there and said to the Lord, "Look, half of my possessions, Lord, I will give to the poor; and if I have defrauded anyone of anything, I will pay back four times as much." ⁹Then Jesus said to him, "Today salvation has come to this house, because he too is a son of Abraham. ¹⁰For the Son of Man came to seek out and to save the lost."* (Lk 19:8–10)

The sacrament of Penance and Reconciliation enacts within us a desire to change our lives and the grace to overcome our sins. If we need to confess the same sins over and over, so be it. It is better to confess the same sins than to have new sins to confess. With patience and trust, in time, we will be better people. It is a journey. And while we walk our way, Jesus comes to heal the wounds of our sins.

To finish your reflection today, I encourage you to plan your next confession, starting with an examination of your conscience and a supplication for the grace of a sincere and true contrition.

Also consider that many saints would have frequent confessions. Would the practice of frequent confessions help give you more strength to overcome your sins? Think about it.

What is the fruit of your reflection today?

_____
_____
_____
_____
_____

Day 5

The sacrament of the Anointing of the Sick is also a sacrament of healing. While the sacrament of Penance and Reconciliation is the spiritual healing of our sins, the Anointing of the Sick is a sacrament for the healing of our illnesses.

Of course, not all illnesses are healed when the sick person receives the sacrament. After all, our final destination is heaven, and physical death is a reality we cannot escape. For this reason, this sacrament also provides the grace of strength, courage, and peace to endure illnesses and as preparation for entering eternal life.

Praying for the sick may not bring physical healing every time, but it can certainly help people manage their condition and help them draw closer to God despite their distress.

Remember that God is merciful and always moved by our needs of healing. In the Old Testament, God reveals Himself as our healer (see Ex 15:26). In the New Testament, Jesus cures a great number of physical afflictions as a sign of the healing of our souls (see the reflections on the topic of healing in Week 3). In the Gospels, Jesus forgives sin and restores people's bodies (see the healing of the paralytic in Mark 2:1–12). Jesus has compassion for all who are afflicted, in their bodies and in their souls.

> *[17]When Jesus heard this, he said to them, "Those who are well have no need of a physician, but those who are sick; I have come to call not the righteous but sinners."* (Mk 2:17)

God showed mercy to the sick in the Old Testament and in the New Testament. Now, in the time of the Church, God continues to be merciful to the sick through the sacraments, especially the Eucharist, the Reconciliation, and the Anointing of the Sick.

Consider the following passages, which describe deeds of the apostles. Notice how healing is presented as a ministry of the Church.

> *[13]They cast out many demons, and anointed with oil many who were sick and cured them.* (Mk 6:13)

> *[17]And these signs will accompany those who believe: by using my name they will cast out demons; they will speak in new tongues; . . . [18c]They will lay their hands on the sick, and they will recover.*
> (Mk 16:17, 18c)

> *[34]Peter said to him, "Aeneas, Jesus Christ heals you; get up and make your bed!" And immediately he got up.* (Acts 9:34)

> *[7]To each is given the manifestation of the Spirit for the common good. . . . [9]to another gifts of healing by the one Spirit.*
> (1 Cor 12:7, 9)

The sacrament of the Anointing of the Sick is performed by the priest. Those who suffer from grave illness or are in danger of death from sickness or old age should call a priest so they can receive the sacrament. The sacrament is a grace for the renewal of faith and trust in the Lord.

> *[14]Are any among you sick? They should call for the elders of the church and have them pray over them, anointing them with oil in the name of the Lord. [15]The prayer of faith will save the sick, and the Lord will raise them up; and anyone who has committed sins will be forgiven.*
> (Jas 5:14–15)

Considering that the sacrament of the Anointing of the Sick is not only for physical illnesses but also for emotional, mental, and spiritual afflictions, what are your thoughts about this sacrament? Have you ever received this sacrament? Have you ever been in a situation in which you could have received it but did not? If yes, why not?

___

___

___

___

I invite you to close this reflection with a prayer.

> Dear Jesus, You are so merciful and compassionate. I am immensely grateful for Your love. You promised to be with me until the end times, and You are fulfilling Your promises through the sacraments. You have been present in my life from the beginning and will be until the end. You received me as one of Yours through Baptism when I started my Christian journey, and You will be there with me to help me prepare for my crossing to the heavenly Promised Land. You gave me the strength I needed through Confirmation, You have nourished me with the Eucharist, and You have healed my soul through Confession. Dear Jesus, come to me with the Anointing of the Sick whenever my body needs healing, and when my time comes, give me the grace to prepare for my final journey with courage and peace. Amen.

What is the fruit of your reflection today?

___

___

___

___

___

Day 6

The last two sacraments, Holy Orders and Matrimony, are related to distinct forms of serving God in the Church. They are special callings to holiness and evangelization, grace for the salvation of others.

Today, let us reflect on the sacrament of Holy Orders, which is a calling for men who are consecrated—that is, set apart for Christ and His Church.

The role of the consecrated priest is very dear to God. In the Old Testament, we find that the tribe of Levi, among the twelve tribes of Israel, was consecrated to God for the service of the whole people. The priests of the Old Testament were responsible for the liturgy and the sacrifices.

In the New Testament, Christ is the high priest of the New Covenant, the one mediator between God and His Church.

> *⁵For there is one God.*
> *There is also one mediator between God and the human race,*
> *Christ Jesus, himself human,*
> *⁶who gave himself as ransom for all.* (1 Tm 2:5–6, *NAB*)

While the priests of the Old Testament had a major responsibility of offering constant sacrifices to God for the people, Christ is the high priest that offered Himself as the divine sacrifice once and for all.

> *¹⁴For by one offering he has made perfect forever those who are being consecrated.* (Heb 10:14, *NAB*)

For this reason, there is no need for animal sacrifices anymore. Replacing the priests of the Old Covenant, the priests of the New

Covenant, acting in the name of Jesus, are called to offer the memorial sacrifice of Christ at every Mass.

> [23c]*The Lord Jesus on the night when he was betrayed took a loaf of bread,* [24]*and when he had given thanks, he broke it and said, "This is my body that is for you. Do this in remembrance of me."* [25]*In the same way he took the cup also, after supper, saying, "This cup is the new covenant in my blood. Do this, as often as you drink it, in remembrance of me."* (1 Cor 11:23c–25)

When Jesus ascended into heaven, He left the twelve apostles (the fulfillment of the twelve tribes of Israel) as the consecrated priests of the New Covenant. Because of them, we can receive the sacraments, especially the Eucharist.

I invite you to take a minute now to ponder the beauty of the Christian priesthood.

The priests are mere human beings, but they represent the Holy One. Despite their faults, they have received authority to forgive our sins, consecrate the Eucharist, and be a visible sign of the presence of Jesus in our midst.

Think about priests from different periods of the history of the Church who have been recognized as saints. I can think of Padre Pio, John Vianney, John Paul II, Augustine, Thomas Aquinas. Can you add some names to this list?

_____

_____

_____

_____

_____

Now think about priests you know who are good men, dedicated to God and His Church, and true role models of service and holiness. I invite you to offer your thanksgiving to God for all these faithful men who said yes to God with their own lives. What is your response to this reflection?

_____

_____

_____

_____

_____

Since the apostles, there has been a line of succession of bishops, through the imposition of hands, that to this day has remained uninterrupted.

Consider the words of Saint Paul to Timothy, who was the first bishop of Ephesus. It seems Saint Paul was a mentor to Timothy, and the gift he mentions in the following passages is the sacrament of Holy Orders.

> *[14]Do not neglect the gift that is in you, which was given to you through prophecy with the laying on of hands by the council of elders.* (1 Tm 4:14)

> *[6]For this reason I remind you to rekindle the gift of God that is within you through the laying on of my hands.* (2 Tm 1:6)

The sacrament of Holy Orders is an apostolic ministry with three different degrees: bishop, priest, and deacon. The Catholic bishops are successors to the apostles.

With the priests and deacons, they share the mission of Christ, serving the Church as pastors of the Christian flock.

Read the encouragement that Peter, as head of the Church, wrote to the priests:

> *[1]Now as an elder myself and a witness of the sufferings of Christ, as well as one who shares in the glory to be revealed, I exhort the elders among you [2]to tend the flock of God that is in your charge, exercising*

the oversight, not under compulsion but willingly, as God would have you do it—not for sordid gain but eagerly. ³Do not lord it over those in your charge, but be examples to the flock. ⁴And when the chief shepherd appears, you will win the crown of glory that never fades away. (1 Pt 5:1–4)

In her history of two thousand years, the Church has sometimes struggled with unfaithful pastors who have wounded Christ's flock. However, Jesus has never abandoned His Church, as He has always been true to His promise, "the gates of Hades will not prevail against it" (Mt 16:18).

When the Church is deeply wounded by sinful pastors, it is a wake-up call for the whole Church to respond with more prayer, interceding for justice, healing, forgiveness, and cleansing and always trusting that the chief Shepherd will take care of His flock.

How do you feel when you hear about the wounds of the Church caused by sinful pastors? I invite you to present your thoughts and feelings to God. And listen. What is God telling you? And what is your response?

_____

_____

_____

_____

_____

The sacrament of Holy Orders is a calling; it is not a career that one chooses. The initiative belongs to Jesus, who picks those He wants.

¹²Now during those days he went out to the mountain to pray; and he spent the night in prayer to God. ¹³And when day came, he called his disciples and chose twelve of them, whom he also named apostles. (Lk 6:12–13)

Do you think Jesus might be calling you? Have you asked Jesus if this vocation is for you?

If this vocation does not apply to you (either because you are a woman or because you have another calling), do you pray often for those who are called? Do you think the Church is in need of holy priests? How do you pray for this?

_____

_____

_____

_____

_____

Priesthood is a calling to holiness, to witness for Christ with the example of a righteous life. The whole Church, including you and me, has the responsibility to pray for the bishops, priests, and deacons so they can be holy and protected from all evil.

Because we live in difficult times, our prayers should be relentless. "Father, give us holy priests. Your will be done according to your word."

Read below what the will of God is, according to His word.

> *⁵I left you behind in Crete for this reason, so that you should put in order what remained to be done, and should appoint elders in every town, as I directed you: ⁶someone who is blameless, married only once, whose children are believers, not accused of debauchery and not rebellious. ⁷For a bishop, as God's steward, must be blameless; he must not be arrogant or quick-tempered or addicted to wine or violent or greedy for gain; ⁸but he must be hospitable, a lover of goodness, prudent, upright, devout, and self-controlled. ⁹He must have a firm grasp of the word that is trustworthy in accordance with the teaching, so that he may be able both to preach with sound doctrine and to refute those who contradict it.* (Ti 1:5–9)

> *⁸Deacons likewise must be serious, not double-tongued, not indulging in much wine, not greedy for money; ⁹they must hold fast to the mystery of the faith with a clear conscience.* (1 Tm 3:8–9)

As you read the passages above, I invite you to consider the Catholic tradition. Except for permanent deacons, who can be married, bishops and priests in the Catholic Church are called to celibacy as a sign of offering their entire selves to Christ.

As a final reflection, ponder this verse from Matthew. Consider how powerful Jesus's calling is and how it prompts such immediate response from those who are called.

> *¹⁹And he said to them, "Follow me, and I will make you fish for people." ²⁰Immediately they left their nets and followed him.* (Mt 4:19–20)

What is the fruit of your reflection today?

_____
_____
_____
_____
_____

Day 7

The sacrament of Matrimony is one of the most beautiful sacraments. The self-giving love of spouses is a sign of the loving relationship between Christ and His Church.

This sacrament was designed by God and is present in the whole history of salvation as a sign of the ultimate plan of God for mankind.

In the beginning of the first book of the Bible, we find Adam and Eve and the first love declaration of mankind, "Bone of my bones,/ and flesh of my flesh" (Gn 2:23). Before the original sin, Adam and Eve, created out of love and for love, lived in perfect harmony, according to God's will.

Let us read this passage:

> ^{27}*God created mankind in his image;*
> *in the image of God he created them;*
> *male and female he created them.*
>
> ^{28}*God blessed them and God said to them: Be fertile and multiply; fill the earth and subdue it.* (Gn 1:27–28, *NAB*)

As we move forward to the last book of the Bible, we find the fulfillment of God's plan in Revelation.

> ^{6}*Then I heard something like the sound of a great multitude or the sound of rushing water or mighty peals of thunder, as they said:*
>
> *"Alleluia!*
> *The Lord has established his reign,*
> *[our] God, the almighty.*
> ^{7}*Let us rejoice and be glad*
> *and give him glory.*

> *For the wedding day of the Lamb has come,*
> *his bride has made herself ready.* (Rev 19:6–7, *NAB*)

What is your reaction as you ponder Matrimony as a sign of the love of Christ for His Church?

_____

_____

_____

_____

_____

Saint Paul, in his letter to the Ephesians, offers a clear understanding of Matrimony as a sign of Christ's love for us. As Jesus gave His life for us, husbands are called to give their lives for their wives. As the Church responds to Jesus in love and respect, wives are called to do the same.

A marriage lived in mutual love and respect is a sacred and powerful testimony of love to the world.

> ^{24}*Just as the church is subject to Christ, so also wives ought to be, in everything, to their husbands.* ^{25}*Husbands, love your wives, just as Christ loved the church and gave himself up for her.* (Eph 5:24–25)

After the fall, Adam and Eve started to experience marital conflicts (see Gn 3:12). That is why couples get married in love but struggle to keep the flame of their love alight.

With the grace of the Holy Spirit given through the sacrament of Matrimony, couples can pray together and ask God for the help they need to overcome their difficulties and heal their wounds.

When a man and a woman get married, two things happen. They get married to each other, and together as a bride, the couple gets married to Christ. This means that husband and wife are never alone in their struggles. For this reason, couples should never forget that Jesus is present in their Matrimony.

Jesus performed His first miracle at a wedding. Remembering that Mary had her part in this miracle too, let us focus now on the fact that Jesus was there, He was present, and He took care of the problem even before the problem was known.

Consider this final piece of the narrative of the wedding at Cana:

> *⁹When the steward tasted the water that had become wine, and did not know where it came from (though the servants who had drawn the water knew), the steward called the bridegroom ¹⁰and said to him, "Everyone serves the good wine first, and then the inferior wine after the guests have become drunk. But you have kept the good wine until now."* (Jn 2:9–10)

Ponder this. The love of the first years of marriage is compared to the good wine that is served first. Problems and wounds harm the love over time, like the inferior wine that is served later, at the risk of running short. However, Jesus wants to keep the good wine until the end.

If you are married, take a moment now to reflect on the kind of wine you have in your marriage at this point. Trust that Jesus wants to keep the good wine until the end. With the help of Mary, talk to Jesus about your marriage and ask Him to bring the best wine.

If you are not married, pray for couples you know who are in need of a better wine. Write down your prayer.

_____
_____
_____
_____
_____

Let us have a final reflection. In the Old Testament, we find several stories, such as that of Tobiah and Sarah (see the book of Tobit), which remind us that love is possible. The book of Songs of Songs is a beautiful collection of love poems. In a literal sense, they reflect the love between spouses. In a spiritual sense, they point to the love between Jesus and His bride.

> *⁶Set me as a seal upon your heart,*
> *as a seal upon your arm;*
> *For Love is strong as Death,*
> *longing is fierce as Sheol.*
> *Its arrows are arrows of fire,*
> *flames of the divine.* (Sg 8:6, *NAB*)

And who is this bride? This bride is our individual souls that long to be united to Christ. This bride is also the Church, as the communion of all souls. And this bride is a couple, a husband and a wife united in Matrimony.

This week, you have reflected on and prayed about the sacraments. You reflected on sacraments as signs of Jesus's presence in the Church. Which sacrament stands out for you? Review your reflections, prayer exercises, and notes from the week and write below what you learned that is new, surprising, or transformative.

_____
_____
_____
_____
_____
_____
_____
_____
_____
_____

Week 8

Church

Every day they devoted themselves to meeting together in the temple area and to breaking bread in their homes. They ate their meals with exultation and sincerity of heart, praising God and enjoying favor with all the people. And every day the Lord added to their number those who were being saved.
(Acts 2:46–47, NAB)

Day 1

In this last week, I invite you to reflect on the Church.

First, I encourage you to think about the Church as an assembly, as the people of God, a community of people united by the same faith in Jesus Christ and bonded to each other by mutual love.

Think of yourself in relation to the Church, not only in terms of "I belong" to the Church but mainly as "I am" the Church, together with all brothers and sisters in faith. Think about the Church as a spiritual building, of which Jesus is the cornerstone and we are the living stones.

> *[11]He is stone rejected by you, the builders, which has become the cornerstone.* (Acts 4:11, NAB)

> *[4]Come to him, a living stone, though rejected by mortals yet chosen and precious in God's sight, and [5]like living stones, let yourselves be built into a spiritual house, to be a holy priesthood, to offer spiritual sacrifices acceptable to God through Jesus Christ.* (1 Pt 2:4–5)

We, the Church, are the visible presence of God in the world. We are the voice, the hands, and the feet of God. We make Him visible to the world through our choices, actions, and the holiness of our testimonies.

Ponder the calling to be the Church. How does your soul react to this?

_____

_____

_____

Now, think about the Church as the Kingdom of God that Jesus announced.

It is a very unique kingdom in many ways. First, it is like a mustard seed (see Mt 13:31–32), as small as twelve uneducated men, but with the help of the Holy Spirit, it grew to spread its branches all over the world.

Second, to be part of this mysterious kingdom, one must be born again through Baptism (see Jn 3:3). Baptism is the entrance to this kingdom.

Also consider that there is a kind of tension about this kingdom. The kingdom is already among us, but at the same time, it has not yet come to its fullness.

> *20 Once Jesus was asked by the Pharisees when the kingdom of God was coming, and he answered, "The kingdom of God is not coming with things that can be observed; 21 nor will they say, 'Look, here it is!' or 'There it is!' For, in fact, the kingdom of God is among you."* (Lk 17:20–21)

The Kingdom of God / Church is already among us, but it still waits for its fulfillment as the new Jerusalem, described by John in his apocalyptic visions of heaven.

The Church, prepared as a bride, will complete her mission in heaven and dwell with God for a glorious eternity.

> *14 For here we have no lasting city, but we are looking for the city that is to come.* (Heb 13:14)

> *1 Then I saw a new heaven and a new earth. The former heaven and the former earth had passed away, and the sea was no more. 2 I also saw the holy city, a new Jerusalem, coming down out of heaven from God, prepared as a bride adorned for her husband. 3 I heard a loud voice from the throne saying, "Behold, God's dwelling is with the human race. He will dwell with them and they will be his people and God himself will always be with them [as their God]. 4 He will wipe*

every tear from their eyes, and there shall be no more death or mourning, wailing or pain, [for] the old order has passed away.
(Rev 21:1–4, *NAB*)

This is the time of the Church, the time between the first and second coming of Christ. This is the time in which we, the Church, are called to announce the gospel to all nations. Meanwhile, we await the glorious manifestation of our Lord and King Jesus Christ.

[15]He said to them, "Go into the whole world and proclaim the gospel to every creature." (Mk 16:15, *NAB*)

Let us review: The Church is the people of God bound by faith, hope, and love. You and I who are baptized are citizens of the Kingdom of God, which is already among us but will be perfected in heaven. Meanwhile, we are called to shine the light of Christ in the world and bring all the nations to the knowledge and acceptance of salvation.

What is your reaction to this?

_____
_____
_____
_____
_____

Let us pray:

> Dear Jesus, thank You for the gift of the Church. Thank You for choosing me to be part of Your kingdom. Thank You for my baptism and for the grace of faith. And thank You for giving me the understanding of my mission in this life while I hope for the new creation in eternity. Thank You for touching my heart right now and giving me the grace of loving Your Church as You love her. Send Your Holy Spirit upon me today so I can have a better under-

standing of the mystery of Your Church. Teach me to love her and care for her as much as You do. Amen.

Continue your prayer, guided by the movements of your heart.

_____
_____
_____
_____
_____

What is the fruit of your reflection today?

_____
_____
_____
_____
_____

Day 2

The Church is One.

In our creed, we profess our faith in the Church, which is One, Holy, Catholic, and Apostolic. Today, let us ponder the Church as One.

The Church is One because Jesus is One. He is One with the Father and the Holy Spirit. And He wants to be united with us, His Church, so that we become One in communion with the Trinity.

I invite you to consider the idea of Church as the mystical body of Christ. Jesus is the one head of a body that has many members, and even though we are many, we become One because He is One.

The idea of unity is very dear to God. Ponder the prayer Jesus spoke at the Last Supper. In such a crucial moment in His life, shortly before His passion, He prays for unity among His disciples and the whole Church.

> [20]*I ask not only on behalf of these, but also on behalf of those who will believe in me through their word,* [21]*that they may all be one. As you, Father, are in me and I am in you, may they also be in us, so that the world may believe that you have sent me.* [22]*The glory that you have given me I have given them, so that they may be one, as we are one,* [23]*I in them and you in me, that they may become completely one, so that the world may know that you have sent me and have loved them even as you have loved me.* [24]*Father, I desire that those also, whom you have given me, may be with me where I am, to see my glory, which you have given me because you loved me before the foundation of the world.* [25]*Righteous Father, the world does not know you, but I know you; and these know that you have sent me.* [26]*I made your name known to them, and I will make it known, so that the love with which you have loved me may be in them, and I in them.* (Jn 17:20–26)

Read the passage again and meditate on the verses that speak to you. Did you notice, in verse 24, that we, the Church, are a gift to Jesus?

Now ponder this: How significant is it that Jesus prayed for unity? How important is unity for you? How can you apply Jesus's wishes to your life? Write down your reflection.

_____

_____

_____

_____

_____

Jesus used the image of the vine and the branches to convey the idea of unity with Him. Jesus was sad because the people of Israel, the chosen people of the Old Covenant, could not accept His message. He insisted that there was no salvation away from Him. He is the way, the truth, and the life (see Jn 14:6).

This message is also for you and for the Church, who is called to remain united with Jesus and with His will and commandments. This is what Jesus said.

> *[1]I am the true vine, and my Father is the vinegrower. [2]He removes every branch in me that bears no fruit. Every branch that bears fruit he prunes to make it bear more fruit. [4]Abide in me as I abide in you. Just as the branch cannot bear fruit by itself unless it abides in the vine, neither can you unless you abide in me. [5]I am the vine, you are the branches. Those who abide in me and I in them bear much fruit, because apart from me you can do nothing. [9]As the Father has loved me, so I have loved you; abide in my love. [10]If you keep my commandments, you will abide in my love, just as I have kept my Father's commandments and abide in his love.* (Jn 15:1–2, 4–5, 9–10)

Being united with Jesus as a branch of the vine is essential, and it inspires us to be personally united with Christ.

However, it is important to go further than that and understand the importance of being united with Jesus as the Church, as His mystical body. In this body, Christ is the head and all members are united with each other through love.

The image of the mystical body is wonderful for understanding that unity with Jesus only makes sense when there is also unity among those who belong to Him.

> *¹I therefore, the prisoner in the Lord, beg you to lead a life worthy of the calling to which you have been called, ²with all humility and gentleness, with patience, bearing with one another in love, ³making every effort to maintain the unity of the Spirit in the bond of peace. ⁴There is one body and one Spirit, just as you were called to the one hope of your calling, ⁵one Lord, one faith, one baptism, ⁶one God and Father of all, who is above all and through all and in all.* (Eph 4:1–6)

> *¹⁸ᵃHe is the head of the body, the church.* (Col 1:18a)

Ponder unity in the Church. What thoughts come to mind when you think about unity among Christians? Have you prayed for unity following the example of Jesus?

_____

_____

_____

_____

_____

The Catholic Church was founded by Jesus Himself and has been faithful to the doctrine received from the apostles since her beginning.

The most important thing that keeps Catholics united is the Eucharist. We are One with Christ as we partake in the One Body of Christ. Through Communion, we become One. Ponder this.

¹⁶The cup of blessing that we bless, is it not a sharing in the blood of Christ? The bread that we break, is it not a sharing in the body of Christ? ¹⁷Because there is one bread, we who are many are one body, for we all partake of the one bread. (1 Cor 10:16–17)

What is the fruit of your reflection today?

_____
_____
_____
_____
_____

Day 3

The Church is Holy.

Just as the Church is One because Jesus is One, the Church is also Holy because Jesus is Holy.

Keep in mind the idea of the Church as the mystical body of Christ. Christ is the head, and we are the members. Even though we are sinners, the Church is Holy because Jesus is Holy. He is the one who sanctifies His Church.

> *²Speak to the whole Israelite community and tell them: Be holy, for I, the LORD your God, am holy.* (Lv 19:2, NAB)

> *⁷Sanctify yourselves, then, and be holy; for I, the LORD, your God, am holy.* (Lv 20:7, NAB)

> *⁴⁸Be perfect, therefore, as your heavenly Father is perfect.* (Mt 5:48)

To be holy is to be perfect, complete, whole, without broken pieces. God created mankind for holiness, to be complete and in complete union with Him, who is Holy.

Sadly, because of the original sin, we are broken, imperfect, and wounded. But the ultimate plan of God for His people is to heal us and bring us to holiness. The members of the Church are holy in the measure of their unity with Jesus.

The Church walks toward her final destination in heaven, when her union with Jesus will be perfected. For now, the Church is Holy because God is Holy, yet she is made up of sinful members until the day God will perfect His work in her.

> ³*Blessed be the God and Father of our Lord Jesus Christ, who has blessed us in Christ with every spiritual blessing in the heavenly places, ⁴just as he chose us in Christ before the foundation of the world to be holy and blameless before him in love. ⁵He destined us for adoption as his children through Jesus Christ, according to the good pleasure of his will, ⁶to the praise of his glorious grace that he freely bestowed on us in the Beloved. ⁷In him we have redemption through his blood, the forgiveness of our trespasses, according to the riches of his grace ⁸that he lavished on us. With all wisdom and insight ⁹he has made known to us the mystery of his will, according to his good pleasure that he set forth in Christ, ¹⁰as a plan for the fullness of time, to gather up all things in him, things in heaven and things on earth.* (Eph 1:3–10)
>
> ²⁵*Husbands, love your wives, just as Christ loved the church and gave himself up for her, ²⁶in order to make her holy by cleansing her with the washing of water by the word, ²⁷so as to present the church to himself in splendor, without a spot or wrinkle or anything of the kind—yes, so that she may be holy and without blemish.* (Eph 5:25–27)

In this life, we cannot be perfect yet. However, by the grace we receive through Christ, we, the Church, can walk toward perfection, collaborating with our faith, hope, humility, prayer, forgiveness, and good deeds.

Ponder this: We are the living stones of a spiritual house that Jesus is preparing for Him. To construct this building, the stones need to be put together with the cement of love. Without love, the building will fall apart.

Think of yourself as a living stone, a member of the mystical body of Christ. Consider love as the measure of holiness.

How much holiness are you bringing to the Church? Are you contributing to make the Church present herself to God "without spot or wrinkle," "holy and without blemish"?

Listen to God about this. What does He say to you? What is your response to God?

_____
_____
_____
_____
_____

God knows our limitations and understands that we are not perfect yet. He looks at us with mercy and compassion and sends His Holy Spirit to work His holiness in us. With humility, we can accept His help and commit to doing our best, hoping to become saints one day.

However, when members of the Church deliberately deviate from God's commandments, they risk creating horrible spots and deep wrinkles in the so-loved bride of Christ.

Consider the sadness in God's heart for the mortal sins committed by members of the Church, especially those who are in leadership positions. Can you feel the hurt in Jesus's heart? What can you do to comfort Jesus?

_____
_____
_____
_____
_____

Between the first and second coming of Christ, the Church was granted a time of preparation, as a bride prepares for her wedding. This is the time we live in now. Concerning this period, Jesus told the parable of the enemy who had planted weeds among a plantation of wheat. When the servants realized this, they wanted to pull the weeds, but the master was wise.

²⁹But he replied, "No; for in gathering the weeds you would uproot the wheat along with them. ³⁰Let both of them grow together until the harvest; and at harvest time I will tell the reapers, Collect the weeds first and bind them in bundles to be burned, but gather the wheat into my barn." (Mt 13:29–30)

This passage from Matthew is a reminder that we should be careful not to condemn the whole Church for the errors of individual members. While we should not allow any form of scandalous sin among us that is deeply hurtful to our brothers and sisters, we are to be careful not to damage the wheat as we attempt to pull the weed. As we recognize the reality of the weed that does not belong, we are not to lose sight of the beauty and splendor of the Church that is made Holy because her beloved is Holy.

Let us finish with a final consideration. The Church is a sign of Christ to the world. The Church is called to announce the gospel with the testimony of her holiness.

Read the following passage, which describes the will of God for the Church as written in a letter from Saint Paul to the Christian community in Colossae. I invite you to open your heart to thanksgiving and intercession for the Church as you read this text.

¹²As God's chosen ones, holy and beloved, clothe yourselves with compassion, kindness, humility, meekness, and patience. ¹³Bear with one another and, if anyone has a complaint against another, forgive each other; just as the Lord has forgiven you, so you also must forgive. ¹⁴Above all, clothe yourselves with love, which binds everything together in perfect harmony. ¹⁵And let the peace of Christ rule in your hearts, to which indeed you were called in the one body. And be thankful. ¹⁶Let the word of Christ dwell in you richly; teach and admonish one another in all wisdom; and with gratitude in your hearts sing psalms, hymns, and spiritual songs to God. ¹⁷And whatever you do, in word or deed, do everything in the name of the Lord Jesus, giving thanks to God the Father through him. (Col 3:12–17)

What is the fruit of your reflection today?

_____
_____
_____
_____
_____

Day 4

The Church is Catholic.

Catholic means universal, total, and whole. The Catholic faith is about truth and love, the most universal core questions of humankind. The Catholic Church is universal for two reasons. First, she has the fullness of salvation, and second, she is for the whole human race.

The Catholic Church has the fullness of salvation as she has preserved the complete doctrine received from the apostles and the Fathers of the Church. The fullness of salvation encompasses the Word of God in the form of scriptures and tradition, the sacraments and sacramentals, the liturgy and the Mass, and the creed and devotions to the Virgin Mary and the saints. All this richness comes from the early Christians, who persevered in the teachings of the apostles. Throughout two thousand years, the bishops, guided by the Holy Spirit, have kept the deposit of faith to this day.

> *^{42}They devoted themselves to the apostles' teaching and fellowship, to the breaking of bread and the prayers. (Acts 2:42)*

> *^{9}Everyone who does not abide in the teaching of Christ, but goes beyond it, does not have God; whoever abides in the teaching has both the Father and the Son. (2 Jn 9)*

> *^{3}For the time is coming when people will not put up with sound doctrine, but having itching ears, they will accumulate for themselves teachers to suit their own desires, ^{4}and will turn away from listening to the truth and wander away to myths. (2 Tm 4:3–4)*

Think about your personal history as a Catholic. Are you a convert or a cradle Catholic? How do you feel about being Catholic? Do you appreciate all the richness of your faith? What do you appreciate the most in the Catholic faith? Do you feel grateful to the bishops, who faithfully persevered in safeguarding the deposit of faith? Stay quiet for a few moments and ponder this. Write down your reflection.

_____
_____
_____
_____

The Catholic Church is catholic because her message is addressed to the totality of mankind—that is, the message is universal, to all peoples, all nations, all times.

> *²⁶For through faith you are all children of God in Christ Jesus. ²⁷For all of you who were baptized into Christ have clothed yourselves with Christ. ²⁸There is neither Jew nor Greek, there is neither slave nor free person, there is not male and female; for you are all one in Christ Jesus. ²⁹And if you belong to Christ, then you are Abraham's descendant, heirs according to the promise.* (Gal 3:26–29, *NAB*)

> *⁹After this I had a vision of a great multitude, which no one could count, from every nation, race, people, and tongue. They stood before the throne and before the Lamb, wearing white robes and holding palm branches in their hands.* (Rev 7:9, *NAB*)

What comes to your mind and soul when you read these passages? Think about it a moment and write down your reflection.

_____
_____
_____
_____

The concept of salvation for all nations was not fully developed until Jesus commanded and the Holy Spirit guided the apostles in missions to all nations.

> *[19]Go therefore and make disciples of all nations, baptizing them in the name of the Father and of the Son and of the Holy Spirit, [20a]and teaching them to obey everything that I have commanded you.*
> (Mt 28:19–20a)

When God called Abraham and revealed Himself as the One God, He said that "all nations" would be blessed in him (see Gn 22:18). However, the Jewish religion was limited to a national practice. It was focused on the Law and the liturgy performed at a local temple. By the time of Jesus, the Jewish faith was centered in the magnificent Temple of Jerusalem, where the priests of the Old Covenant offered daily sacrifices for the sins of the people.

Once the history of salvation came to its culmination in Jesus Christ, we received salvation through His blood. Jesus is the sacrifice of redemption for all mankind. Therefore, there is no more need for the sacrifice of animals. Since the main purpose of the temple was to offer sacrifices, there is no more need of a temple.

> *[11]But when Christ came as high priest of the good things that have come to be, passing through the greater and more perfect tabernacle not made by hands, that is, not belonging to this creation, [12]he entered once for all into the sanctuary, not with blood of goats and calves but with his own blood, thus obtaining eternal redemption.*
> (Heb 9:11–12, NAB)

The Temple of Jerusalem was destroyed in 70 AD and never rebuilt. Why? Because Jesus is the true Temple, with no walls, no frontiers, and no restrictions. In Him, the one perfect sacrifice for all was completed.

> *[22]I saw no temple in the city, for its temple is the Lord God almighty and the Lamb.* (Rev 21:22, NAB)

Consider this: Jesus is our true Temple; it is through Him, in Him, and with Him that we approach God to worship and offer our lives as living sacrifices.

Now when we build churches all over the world, we have the understanding that they are sacred places to gather together as people of God, to worship and celebrate salvation with thanksgiving and communion. The churches, where the Blessed Sacrament dwells in the tabernacle, are welcoming places for all. They are sacred signs of a reality that tells of eternal salvation for all peoples through Christ our Lord.

As a final reflection, I invite you to ponder the following passage and consider what God is telling you personally.

> [19]*So then you are no longer strangers and aliens, but you are citizens with the saints and also members of the household of God,* [20]*built upon the foundation of the apostles and prophets, with Christ Jesus himself as the cornerstone.* [21]*In him the whole structure is joined together and grows into a holy temple in the Lord;* [22]*in whom you also are built together spiritually into a dwelling place for God.* (Eph 2:19–22)

> [16]*Do you not know that you are God's temple and that God's Spirit dwells in you?* (1 Cor 3:16)

What is the fruit of your reflection today?

_____
_____
_____
_____
_____

Day 5

The Church is Apostolic.

The Church is apostolic because she has the apostles as her foundation. All the Church, including you and me, is apostolic in the sense that we are sent to evangelize. However, a few members are chosen to keep the unity of the Church and preserve the teaching of the apostles.

There is no nation without a leader, or community swimming pool without a director, or school without a principal. Because Jesus cared about His Church, He picked the twelve apostles to be in charge and guide the Church. They are the foundation of the Church, with Peter as the rock. The walls of the New Jerusalem in heaven, as described in the book of Revelation, will celebrate this.

> *^{14}The wall of the city had twelve courses of stones as its foundation, on which were inscribed the twelve names of the twelve apostles of the Lamb.* (Rev 21:14, NAB)

In the Kingdom of God, Jesus is the King and Peter has the role of His prime minister, responsible for the keys and in charge of the kingdom's affairs until the King returns. To Peter was given the necessary authority to keep the Church united in Christ as one body.

> *^{18}And I tell you, you are Peter, and on this rock I will build my church, and the gates of Hades will not prevail against it. ^{19}I will give you the keys of the kingdom of heaven, and whatever you bind on earth will be bound in heaven, and whatever you loose on earth will be loosed in heaven.* (Mt 16:18–19)

Consider the Church as a flock of sheep that needs a shepherd. Without a shepherd, the sheep go astray. Jesus is the Good Shepherd (see Jn 10:11), but Peter was the one Jesus asked to take care of the sheep for Him.

> *[15]When they had finished breakfast, Jesus said to Simon Peter, "Simon son of John, do you love me more than these?" He said to him, "Yes, Lord; you know that I love you." Jesus said to him, "Feed my lambs."* (Jn 21:15)

Why do you think Jesus chose the apostles to be in charge of the Church, with Peter as their leader? What are your thoughts about the bishops' leadership? What are your thoughts about the role of the Pope in the Church? Why is this important?

_____
_____
_____
_____
_____

At this point, you have probably noticed that the characteristics of the Church (One, Holy, Catholic, and Apostolic) are inseparable and complement each other. Being apostolic preserves the unity of the one Church, which is the essence of being catholic, while the fullness of being catholic is the way to holiness.

I invite you to close your reflection today by meditating on each phrase of the summary of our faith, as stated in the Nicene Creed. Take some time to pray sentence by sentence, staying with each as long as you need and pondering the beauty and mystery of our faith.

> We believe in one God,
> the Father, the Almighty,
> maker of heaven and earth,
> and of all that is, seen and unseen.

We believe in one Lord, Jesus Christ,
the only Son of God,
eternally begotten of the Father,
God from God, Light from Light,
true God from true God,
begotten, not made,
one in Being with the Father.
Through him all things were made.
For us men and for our salvation,
he came down from heaven:

by the power of the Holy Spirit
he was born of the Virgin Mary,
and became man.

For our sake he was crucified
under Pontius Pilate;
he suffered died and was buried.

On the third day he rose again
in fulfillment of the Scriptures;

he ascended into heaven
and is seated at the right hand of the Father.
He will come again in glory
to judge the living and the dead,
and his kingdom will have no end.

We believe in the Holy Spirit,
the Lord, the giver of life,
who proceeds from the
Father and the Son.
With the Father and the Son
he is worshipped and glorified.
He has spoken through the Prophets.
We believe in one holy
catholic and apostolic Church.

We acknowledge one
baptism for the forgiveness of sins.
We look for the resurrection of the dead,
and the life of the world to come.
Amen.
(*CCC*)

Which part of the creed calls your attention today? Does it feel right to affirm your faith? Why? If you have questions, have you considered talking about it with someone you trust? Have you considered praying and asking God to show you the fullness of the truth?

_____
_____
_____
_____
_____

What is the fruit of your reflection today?

_____
_____
_____
_____
_____

Day 6

The Church is our Mother.

Within her, we feel protected, as Noah's family was protected from the great flood (see Gn 7:23). Like a mother, the Church thinks of you and longs for you with Jesus, who said:

> *[37]Jerusalem, Jerusalem, the city that kills the prophets and stones those who are sent to it! How often have I desired to gather your children together as a hen gathers her brood under her wings, and you were not willing!* (Mt 23:37)

Jesus knows better than any of us what it is to be taken care of by a most loving mother. The child Jesus experienced the tenderness and protection of Mary and wanted us to have her love in our spiritual pilgrimage. I wonder if Jesus also thought about Mary when He said to His disciples in Jn 14:18 (*NAB*), "I will not leave you orphans." On the cross, Jesus gave us an additional precious gift.

> [26] *When Jesus saw his mother and the disciple whom he loved standing beside her, he said to his mother, "Woman, here is your son."* [27]*Then he said to the disciple, "Here is your mother." And from that hour the disciple took her into his own home.* (Jn 19:26–27)

From a literal sense, we understand that Jesus was making sure His mother and His beloved disciple would take care of each other. From a spiritual sense, this is Jesus, first, referring to you and, second, to the whole Church.

Every one of Jesus's words has a profound meaning. Knowing He was thinking of you on the cross, how do you feel when you read again the passage above and listen to Jesus talking to you directly?

How is your relationship with Mary? Did you take her home with you?

_____

_____

_____

_____

It also makes sense to understand Mary as the mother of the whole Church. She carried Jesus in her womb, took care of Him, protected Him, and stayed with Him to the end. This spiritual mother also embraces the Church that is the mystical body of Christ. She was present on the day the Church was born and will be present at the end of times.

Read the following two passages. One refers to the birth of the Church, and the second relates to the events of the end of ages.

> [14] *All these were constantly devoting themselves to prayer, together with certain women, including Mary the mother of Jesus, as well as his brothers.* (Acts 1:14)

> [1] *A great sign appeared in the sky, a woman clothed with the sun, with the moon under her feet, and on her head a crown of twelve stars.* (Rev 12:1, NAB)

Mary, the new Eve, was present when the Church, the new creation, was born. She continues to be present in the Church, interceding for us as she did at the wedding at Cana (see Jn 2:1–10).

Mary is our mother and our queen, the queen of the whole Church, holding a very special place in the Kingdom of God. Mary is the fulfillment of the queen mother of King Solomon.

> [20]*Then she said, "I have one small request to make of you; do not refuse me." And the king said to her, "Make your request, my mother; for I will not refuse you."* (1 Kgs 2:20)

Have you ever paid attention to the words of the Hail Holy Queen prayer? In this prayer, the Church identifies with Israel, the people of God of the Old Covenant, and contemplates the salvation pilgrimage. We ask Mary to be with us in our journey through this land of exile and take us home to our destiny in heaven.

Mary takes care of the Church as a mother prepares her daughter for her wedding day. The mother of the bride is not the one who walks the bride down the aisle. She puts herself aside so the bride and groom can be the center of attention. However, the mother of the bride is the one who has given birth to the girl, raised her, taken care of her for years, and finally, she is the one who prepares and makes the arrangements for the wedding. The mother of the bride is present, but she steps aside and it is her joy to point to the bride and groom.

The words of John the Baptist, like the best man's, emphasize that the bride and groom are the ones at the heart of the wedding.

> ^{29}*He who has the bride is the bridegroom. The friend of the bridegroom, who stands and hears him, rejoices greatly at the bridegroom's voice. For this reason my joy has been fulfilled.* (Jn 3:29)

> ^{6}*Then I heard something like the sound of a great multitude or the sound of rushing water or mighty peals of thunder, as they said:*
> *"Alleluia!*
> *The Lord has established his reign,*
> *[our] God, the almighty.*
> ^{7}*Let us rejoice and be glad*
> *and give him glory,*
> *For the wedding day of the Lamb has come,*
> *his bride has made herself ready.*
> ^{8}*She was allowed to wear*
> *a bright, clean linen garment."* (Rev 19:6–8, *NAB*)

Consider this: The Church is the bride. You are the bride. Jesus is the bridegroom. Jesus wants to be united with you today and to fulfill this union when the time comes.

Mary makes herself present to bring you to Jesus today. At the end, on the wedding day, Mary will be there to rejoice with you. Can you perceive her silent presence?

_____
_____
_____
_____

How important is Mary to you as a mother who takes you to Jesus and makes you ready for the wedding? Considering your spiritual journey, what can you tell Mary? Do you have difficulties talking to her? If you do, ask Jesus to reveal to you what He thinks about it; then try and talk to Mary.

_____
_____
_____
_____

What is the fruit of your reflection today?

_____
_____
_____
_____

Day 7

The Church is on a journey.

Therefore, to be the Church is to be on a journey, in pilgrimage to enter more and more into friendship with God, until a complete union has been fulfilled. Today, let us ponder being on a journey.

Consider Abraham, the first one to be called.

> *^{1}The LORD said to Abram: Go forth from your land, your relatives, and from your father's house to a land that I will show you. . . .*
>
> *^{4a}Abram went as the LORD directed him.*
> (Genesis 12:1, 4a, NAB)

In Isaiah 41:8, God called Abraham his friend. Abraham believed in God, and his faith inspired him to change the course of his life, in complete trust in God and His promises. His starting point was the detachment from all that was familiar to him. In the same way, our quest to enter into friendship with God starts with a detachment from sins and old habits of the past and a firm decision to accept a new way of life.

> *^{17}Now this I affirm and insist on in the Lord: you must no longer live as the Gentiles live, in the futility of their minds. ^{18}They are darkened in their understanding, alienated from the life of God because of their ignorance and hardness of heart. ^{19}They have lost all sensitivity and have abandoned themselves to licentiousness, greedy to practice every kind of impurity. ^{20}That is not the way you learned Christ! ^{21}For surely you have heard about him and were taught in him, as truth is in Jesus. ^{22}You were taught to put away your former way of life, your old self, corrupt and deluded by its lusts, ^{23}and to be renewed in the spirit*

of your minds, ²⁴and to clothe yourselves with the new self, created according to the likeness of God in true righteousness and holiness.
(Eph 4:17–24)

As we progress through our journey, we find Moses as another inspiration. In Exodus 33:11 (*NAB*), "The LORD used to speak to Moses face to face, as a person speaks to a friend." Moses talked to God and listened to God. Their relationship was developed as they spent time together.

Once we have accepted the renewal of our lives and decided to be friends with God, it is important to persevere in continued prayer, meditation on the Word of God, and service for the love of Christ.

It is during this part of the journey that we are tested. Here, perseverance is key; it is required for a long walk, sometimes longer than we would wish. Praying and searching for God, over and over, seeking the face of God that pours His grace and shows His love but sometimes disappears.

This path is not a straight line. It is like the pilgrimage of Israel through the wilderness. During this part of the journey, your longing for God is your only strength to overcome the trials.

> *[1]My child, when you come to serve the Lord,*
> *prepare yourself for trials.*
> *[2]Be sincere of heart and steadfast,*
> *and do not be impetuous in time of adversity.*
> *[3]Cling to him, do not leave him,*
> *that you may prosper in your last days.*
> *[4]Accept whatever happens to you;*
> *in periods of humiliation be patient.*
> *[5]For in fire gold is tested,*
> *and the chosen, in the crucible of humiliation.*
> *[6]Trust in God, and he will help you;*
> *make your ways straight and hope in him.* (Sir 2:1–6, *NAB*)

Finally, the journey leads us to the living waters that the Samaritan woman wished to drink (see Jn 4). Here, the key is grace, and the initiative belongs to God. One can only desire, persevere, and hope to say, as Saint Paul did,

> [20]*And it is no longer I who live, but it is Christ who lives in me. And the life I now live in the flesh I live by faith in the Son of God, who loved me and gave himself for me.* (Gal 2:20)

The journey you are finishing today is just one among many you are called to take. Each one will lead you to ever deeper levels of relationship with God. Yet every time, faith, prayer, detachment from your own will, and openness to grace for a transformed life seem to summarize the ever-deeper path for entering into friendship with God.

This is the path that Mary and the saints walked. This is the path you are called to continue on, embracing the tension between already being in the presence of God but not being entirely there yet.

You are called to be in this constant movement of approaching God with faith; talking and listening to Him; opening up to love, nourished by the grace of the sacraments; and hoping for the joy of the final and complete encounter with Jesus, the bridegroom.

May you join the bride Church to ask Jesus to come today into your heart. May He come today and tomorrow and at the last day.

> [17]*The Spirit and the bride say, "Come." Let the hearer say, "Come." Let the one who thirsts come forward, and the one who wants it receive the gift of life-giving water.* (Rev 22:17, NAB)

Now, let us wrap up this journey with a final reflection. Today, you are completing an eight-week journey of daily reflections as you seek to enter into friendship with God. I invite you to take some time to review your walk through this journey and evaluate your growth. Go back through your notes. Write down the impressions you have now about what you wrote then, as you reflected and prayed about Praise,

Forgiveness, Healing, Prayer, Word of God, Service, Sacraments, and finally the Church.

_____
_____
_____
_____
_____
_____

In which topic did you notice the most growth? Do you feel more familiar with sacred scriptures? Do you feel growth in your prayer? Do you have a better understanding of the presence of Jesus in the sacraments? Do you feel more meaning in being the Church? Do you feel your friendship with God has moved up to the next level?

_____
_____
_____
_____
_____
_____

Finally, what is your next step in your continued journey to enter into friendship with God? Are you ready to be a beloved of Jesus?

_____
_____
_____
_____

_____

_____

_____

Let us conclude with a final prayer:

> Dear Jesus, thank You for this opportunity to grow in knowledge and intimacy with You. I ask Your blessings for my continued journey as I hope to be closer to You and let You lead the way. Thank You for calling me to enter into friendship with You, and for giving me the grace to accept this calling. Thank You for calling me not just into a friendship with you but into a relationship of love, as that of a bride with her bridegroom. Thank you for making me your beloved. Give me the grace to understand the depth and joy of this calling as I say yes to you today and forever. Amen.